THE MUSES ARE HEARD

An Account by

TRUMAN CAPOTE

On Monday, December 19, 1955, two dogs and ninety-four Americans, all members of the U. S. production, Porgy and Bess, left East Berlin to travel by train to Leningrad, U.S.S.R., where the opera was to have its Russian premiere. This was the first American theatrical company ever to invade the Soviet Union, an event destined to receive world-wide attention. Mr. Capote, whose narrative covers the eight-day period between the Berlin departure and Leningrad premiere, accompanied the train for the purpose of recording the intimate aspects of a cultural exchange. Here it is: a swift, startling, factual account that reads like a novel.

"wicked, witty, and utterly devastating."
—Sterling North

"absorbing reading from the first moment."
—Harper's Magazine

"a wise and witty report on Russia."
—Time

"reads much like a novel—and a first-class one." —San Francisco Examiner

MODERN LIBRARY PAPERBACKS *are published by Random House in order to make the best books of all times available to the public at a price it can readily afford.*

An Account by TRUMAN CAPOTE

The Muses
Are Heard

PUBLISHED BY RANDOM HOUSE
New York

Portions of this book appeared originally
in *The New Yorker* in different form

Random House IS THE PUBLISHER OF *The Modern Library*

BENNETT CERF · DONALD S. KLOPFER

Manufactured in the United States of America by H. Wolff

for Barbara Paley

Part I

When the Cannons Are Silent

On Saturday, the seventeenth of December, 1955, a foggy wet day in West Berlin, the cast of the American production, *Porgy and Bess,* and others associated with the company, a total of ninety-four persons, were asked to assemble at the company's rehearsal hall for a "briefing" to be conducted by Mr. Walter N. Walmsley, Jr., and Mr. Roye L. Lowry, respectively Counsel and Second Secretary of the American Embassy in Moscow. Mr. Walmsley and Mr. Lowry had traveled from Moscow expressly to advise and answer any questions members of the production might have concerning their forthcoming appearance in Leningrad and Moscow.

This trip to Russia, the first of its kind ever attempted by an American theatrical group, was to be the culmination of a four-year world tour for *Porgy and Bess.* It had come about after many months of complicated, in some areas still beclouded, negotiation between the U.S.S.R. and the producers of the Gershwin opera, Robert Breen and Blevins Davis, who operate under the name Everyman Opera, Incorporated.

Although the Russians had not yet delivered their actual visas, the enormous troupe, consisting of fifty-eight actors, seven backstage personnel, two conductors, assorted wives and office workers, six children and their schoolteacher, three journalists, two dogs and one psychiatrist, were all set to depart within the next forty-eight hours, traveling by train from East Berlin via Warsaw and Moscow to Leningrad, a distance of some eleven hundred miles, yet requiring, apparently, three days and nights.

On my way to the diplomatic briefing, I shared a taxi with Mrs. Ira Gershwin and a square-cut, muscular man called Jerry Laws, who was formerly a boxer and is presently a singer. Mrs. Gershwin is of course the wife of the lyricist who, aside from being the brother of its composer, is himself co-author of *Porgy and Bess*. Periodically, for the past four years, she has left her husband at home in Beverly Hills to accompany the opera on its around-the-world wanderings: "Ira's such a stick-in-the-mud. He hates to go from one room to the next. But I'm a gypsy, darling. I love wheels." Known to her friends as Lee, an abbreviation of Lenore, she is a small and fragile woman devoted to diamonds, and wears them, quite a few, at both breakfast and dinner. She has sun-streaked hair and a heart-shaped face. The flighty fragments of her conversation, delivered in a girlish voice that rushes along in an unsecretive whisper, are pasted together with terms of endearment.

"Oh, love," she said, as we rode through the dark drizzle along the Kurfurstendam, "have you heard about the Christmas tree? The Russians are giving us a Christmas tree. In Leningrad. I think that's so sweet of them. Since they don't *believe* in Christmas. They don't—do they, darling? Anyway, their Christmas comes much later. Because they have a different calendar. Darling, do you think it's true?"

4

"About whether they believe in Christmas?" said Jerry Laws.

"*No*, love," said Mrs. Gershwin impatiently. "About the microphones. And the photographs."

For several days there had been speculation among the company on the subject of personal privacy in Russia. It was based on the rumor that their letters would be censored, their hotel rooms wired and the walls encrusted with concealed cameras.

After a thoughtful moment, Laws said, "I believe it."

"Oh, darling, you don't!" Mrs. Gershwin protested. "It can't be true! After all, *where* are we going to gossip? Unless we simply stand in the bathroom and keep flushing. As for the cameras—"

"I believe that, too," said Laws.

Mrs. Gershwin settled into a musing silence until we reached the street where the rehearsal hall was located. Then, rather wistfully, she said, "I *still* think it's nice about the Christmas tree."

We were five minutes late, and had difficulty in finding seats among the folding chairs that had been set up at one end of the mirrored rehearsal hall. It was crowded and the room was well heated; nevertheless many of those present, as though they could feel already the cold winds of the steppes, sat bundled in the paraphernalia, the scarves and wooly coats, they'd specially acquired for their Russian journey. A competitive spirit had pervaded the purchasing of these

5

outfits, of which more than several had a certain Eskimo-look.

The meeting was called to order by Robert Breen. In addition to being the co-producer of *Porgy and Bess,* he is also its director. After he'd introduced the representatives from the Moscow Embassy, Mr. Walmsley and Mr. Lowry, who were seated behind a table facing us, Mr. Walmsley, a stocky middle-aged man with a Mencken-style haircut and a dry, drawling manner, began by speaking of the "unique opportunity" the proposed tour offered and congratulating the company in advance on the "great success" he was sure they would have behind the iron curtain.

"Since nothing happens in the Soviet Union that isn't planned, and since it is *planned* that you should have a success there, I feel perfectly safe in congratulating you now."

As though sensing a faultiness in his colleague's presumed compliment, Mr. Lowry, a youngish man with the strait-laced façade of a schoolmaster, interposed to suggest that while what Mr. Walmsley had said was perfectly correct, it was also true that there was "a genuine excitement in Russia about your coming there. They know the Gershwin music. In fact, a Russian acquaintance of mine told me he was at a party the other night where three friends of his sang 'Bess, You Is My Woman Now' all the way through."

The cast smiled appreciatively, and Mr. Walmsley resumed. "Yes, there are some nice Russians. Very nice people. But they have a bad government," he said, in slow, spelling-it-out tones. "You must always bear in mind that their system of government is basically hostile to our own. It is a system, with rules and regulations, such as you have never experienced before. Certainly in my experience, which is a long one, I've never encountered anything like it."

A member of the cast, John McCurry, raised his hand to ask a question. McCurry plays the villainous part of Crown, and is, in his own appearance, high and heavy and somewhat forbidding, as befits the role. He wanted to know, "Suppose some of these people invite us into their home? See, most places we go, people do that. Now, is it all right for us to go?"

The two diplomats exchanged an amused glance. "As you may well imagine," said Mr. Walmsley, "we at the Embassy have never been bothered with that problem. We're never invited *any*where. Except officially. I can't say *you* won't be. And if so, by all means take advantage of the opportunity. From what I understand," he continued, "your hosts plan an extensive program of entertainment. Something every minute. Enough to wear you out."

Some of the youngsters smacked their lips at this prospect, but one of them complained, "I don't touch a drop of nothing. So when they're making all these toasts we've heard about, how do I get out of it gracefully?"

Mr. Walmsley shrugged. "You don't have to drink if you don't want to."

"Sure, man," the worried one was advised by a

friend, "nobody's got to drink what they don't want to. And what you don't want, you hand to me."

Now the questions came quickly. The parents, for instance, were concerned about their children. Would there be pasteurized milk? Yes. Still, Mr. Lowry thought it advisable to take a supply of Starlac, which is what he fed his own two children. And the water, was it fit to drink? Perfectly safe. Mr. Walmsley often drank it from the tap. How does one address a Soviet citizen? "Well," said Mr. Walmsley, "I *wouldn't* call them Comrade. Mr. and Mrs. will do." What about shopping, was it expensive? "Outrageously," but it hardly mattered, since there was nothing much to buy anyway. How cold did it get? Oh, it *could* occasionally go to thirty-two below zero. In that case, would their hotel room be warm? Yes, indeed. Overheated, actually.

When these fundamentals had been gone through, a voice from the back raised itself to say, "There's been so much myth talk around here. We heard we're going to be trailed all the time."

"Trailed?" Mr. Walmsley smiled. "Perhaps. Though not in the manner you're thinking of. If they assign anyone to follow you, it will be for your own protection. You must, you see, expect to attract extraordinary attention, crowds wherever you go. It won't be like walking down a street in Berlin. For that reason you may be followed, yes."

"After all," said Mr. Lowry, "the Ministry of Culture has been so anxious to have you come there that you will probably receive very generous treatment, free of the niggling-naggling that a stray foreign visitor might expect."

The voice from the back persisted, somewhat in a key of disappointment. "We heard they going to trail us. And open our letters."

"Ah," said Mr. Walmsley, "*that* is another matter. Something you take for granted. I always assume my letters have been opened."

His audience shifted in their chairs, their eyes swerving with I-told-you-so's. Robert Breen's secretary, Nancy Ryan, stood up. Miss Ryan (Radcliffe '52) had been with the company three months, having taken the job because of an interest in the theatre. A New Yorker, she is blonde, very blue-eyed, tall, just under six feet in fact, and bears considerable resemblance to her mother, an often-photographed and celebrated beauty, Mrs. William Rhinelander Stewart. She wanted to make a suggestion. "Mr. Walmsley, if it's true our letters will be censored, then wouldn't it be better to do all our correspondence on post cards? I mean, if they didn't have to open it to read it, wouldn't that cause less of a delay in outgoing mail?"

Mr. Walmsley seemed not to think Miss Ryan's plan had much merit, as either a time-saving or trouble-saving device. Meanwhile, Mrs. Gershwin had been urging Jerry Laws into action. "Go on, darling. Ask him about the microphones."

Laws caught the diplomat's attention. "A lot of us," he said, "we've been worried about the possibility of wire-tapping in our rooms."

Mr. Walmsley nodded. "I should say it's more than a possibility. Again, it's the sort of thing you should assume. Of course, no one really *knows*."

There was a silent pause, during which Mrs. Gershwin, plucking at a diamond brooch, seemed to wait for Jerry Laws to bring up the matter of concealed cameras, but he hadn't the chance before McCurry regained the floor.

McCurry leaned forward, hunching his burly shoulders. He said he thought it was about time they stopped beating around the bush and came to grips with "the big problem. The big problem is, now what do we say when they ask us political stuff? I'm speaking of the Negro situation."

McCurry's deep voice made the question ride across the room like a wave, collecting as it went the complete interest of the audience. Mr. Walmsley hesitated, as though uncertain whether to ride over it or swim under; at all events, he seemed not prepared to meet it head on.

"You don't have to answer political questions, any more than they would answer questions of that nature put to them by you." Walmsley cleared his throat, and added, "It's all dangerous ground. Treading on eggs."

Mutterings in the audience indicated that they felt

the diplomat's advice was inadequate. Lowry whispered in Walmsley's ear, and McCurry consulted his wife, a melancholy woman who was sitting beside him with their three-year-old daughter on her lap. Then McCurry said, "But they're bound to ask us about the Negro situation. They always do. Last year we were in Yugoslavia, and all the time we were there—"

"Yes, I know," said Walmsley peremptorily. "That's what this whole thing is about. That's the point, isn't it?"

Walmsley's statement, or possibly the manner in which it was made, seemed to rub several people the wrong way; and Jerry Laws, a legend in the company for his fighting quick temper, jumped to his feet, his body stiff with tension. "Then how do we handle it? Should we answer it the way it is? Tell the truth? Or do you want us to gloss it over?"

Walmsley blinked. He took off a pair of horn-rimmed glasses and polished them with a handkerchief. "Why, tell the truth," he said. "Believe me, sir, the Russians know as much about the Negro situation as you do. And they don't give a damn one way or another. Except for statements, propaganda, anything they can turn to their own interests. I think you ought to keep in mind that any interviews you give will be picked up by the American press and reprinted in your home-town newspapers."

A woman, the first who had spoken, rose from her seat in the front row. "We all know there's discrimination back home,'' she said in a shy voice to which everyone listened respectfully. "But in the last eight years Negroes have made a lot of progress. We've come a long way and that's the truth. We can point with pride to our scientists, artists. If we did that (in Russia), it might do a lot of good.''

Others agreed, and addressed the group in a similar vein. Willem Van Loon, a Russian-speaking son of the late historian, and one of the persons handling publicity for Everyman Opera, announced that he was "very, very glad this matter is being gone into so thoroughly. The other day I had a couple of the cast taping an interview for the American Service stations here in Germany, and touching on this point, this racial question, I knew we had to be very, very careful, because of being so near to East Berlin and the possibility of our being monitored—''

"Of course,'' said Walmsley, quietly interrupting. "I suppose you realize that we're being monitored right now.''

Clearly Van Loon had not, nor had anyone else, to judge from the general consternation and gazing-round to see who could be the cause of Walmsley's remark. But any evidence, at least in the shape of mysterious strangers, was not apparent. Van Loon, however, didn't finish what he'd intended saying. His voice trailed away, as did the meeting itself, which shortly came to a meandering conclusion. Both of the diplomats blushed when the company thanked them with applause.

"Thank you," said Walmsley. "It's been a great pleasure to talk to you. Mr. Lowry and I don't often get into contact with the atmosphere of grease paint."

The director, Robert Breen, then called his cast to rehearsal, but before it began, there was much milling about and swapping of opinions on the "briefing." Jerry Laws restricted himself to one word, "Uninformative." Mrs. Gershwin, on the contrary, seemed to have found it too informative. "I'm stunned, darling. Think of living like that! Always assuming. Never *knowing*. Seriously, darling, where are we going to gossip?"

Downstairs, I was offered a return ride to the hotel by Warner Watson, production assistant to Mr. Breen. He introduced me to Dr. Fabian Schupper, who also shared the taxi. Dr. Schupper is an American student at the German Psychoanalytic Institute. I was told he'd been invited on the Russian tour to counteract any "stresses" members of the company might experience. At the last moment, much to his disappointment, Dr. Schupper did not actually go, the management having decided that a psychiatrist was perhaps, after all, not necessary; though the fact that psychoanalysis and its practitioners are not welcome in the Soviet Union may well have been a contributing cause. But at the moment, in the taxi, he was advising Warner Watson to "relax."

Watson, lighting a cigarette with hands that trembled noticeably, said, "Relaxed people do *not* get productions like this played on the samovar circuit."

Watson is in his late thirties. He has a graying crew-cut, and timid, resigned brown eyes. There is about his face, and his manner too, a blurred gentleness, a beyond-his-years fatigue. At one time an actor, he has been associated with Everyman Opera since its inception in 1952. In his job, he is primarily concerned with what he calls "fencing things in." During the past two weeks in Berlin, he'd very nearly taken up residence at the Soviet Embassy, attempting to get a few things fenced in. Despite these efforts, there remained a multiplicity of matters that had escaped corralling. Among them, there was the situation over the company's passports, which, at this late date, were still lurking in Russian hands waiting to be visaed. Then, too, Watson was encountering trouble on the subject of the train by which the troupe was to travel to Leningrad. The production had requested four sleeping cars. The Russians had replied, quite flatly, that they could only supply three second-class cars with "soft-bed" (the Russian term for sleeping berth) accommodations. These, together with a baggage car and a car for the show's scenery, would be attached to The Blue Express, a regularly scheduled Soviet train running between East Berlin and Moscow. Watson's difficulty was that he could not obtain from the Russians a plan of the "soft-bed" cars, and so was unable to chart out sleeping arrangements. He therefore imagined on the train a slapstick *Walpurgisnacht*: "More bodies than berths." He'd also not been able to learn at what hotels in either Leningrad or Moscow the troupe would be staying, and other details of that nature. "They'll never tell you the whole thing about anything. Not all at once. *If* they tell you A, they *might* tell you B, but between the two there's a long, long wait."

Apparently, though, the Russians themselves did not practice the same patience they required of others. Some hours earlier a cable had arrived from Moscow that Watson counted among the causes for his trembling hands. UNLESS ORCHESTRATIONS DELIVERED EMBASSY BERLIN TONIGHT WILL POSTPONE LENINGRAD OPENING REDUCE FEE. The Soviets had for weeks been demanding the orchestrations because they wanted their musicians to rehearse in advance of the company's arrival. Breen, fearing the orchestrations, his only copy, might be lost in transit, had refused to comply. But this ultimatum cable, with its two dire last words, seemed to have changed his mind, and now Watson was on his way to deliver the orchestrations to the Soviet Embassy.

"Don't worry," said Watson, wiping beads of moisture from his upper lip. "*I'm* not worried. We're going to get all this fenced in."

"Relax," said Dr. Schupper.

Back at my hotel, the Kempenski, where many of the company were staying, I stopped by Breen's suite to see his wife, Wilva. She'd just returned from an

15

overnight flight to Brussels, where she'd gone to consult a doctor. For some while twinges of appendicitis had been troubling her, and when, the day before, she'd flown to Brussels, it was with the knowledge that she might have to undergo an immediate operation, thereby canceling her part in the trip to Russia. The previous October she'd spent ten days in Moscow discussing arrangements for the tour with the Ministry of Culture, a "fascinating" experience that had made her anxious to return.

"It's all right, the doctor says I can go. I didn't know how much I wanted to until I thought I couldn't," she said, smiling the smile that seems less an expression than a circumstance of her eager, her anxious-to-please personality. Mrs. Breen has dimples and large brown eyes. Her hair, a maple color, is worn upswept and held in place by huge pins that could serve as weapons. At the moment, she was wearing a dress of purple wool, the color that dominates her wardrobe: "Robert's mad for purple." She and Breen met at the University of Minnesota, where both were graduate students in the drama department. They have been married eighteen years. Though Mrs. Breen has played professionally on the stage, once as Shakespeare's Juliet, her real devotions, in the words of one of their associates, are to "Robert and Robert's career. If she could find enough paper, she'd wrap up the world and hand it to him."

On the surface of it, a shortage of paper would not

series of pleading trips to Washington, that he could no longer rely on the patronage of his Potomac friends. Apparently they thought his project too unprecedented, or, in their own phrase, "politically premature." In other words, not one cent.

In New York, theatrical circles theorized that the State Department had withdrawn its support because they feared the opera too vulnerable to the purposes of Soviet propaganda. Defenders of the enterprise considered this attitude nonsensical. In their opinion, the fact that such social-critical aspects as the opera contained could be freely presented in the American theatre counteracted the possibilities of effective propaganda on that score. A further argument was that in Russia the very presence of the Negro cast, their affluent appearance, their so obviously unoppressed outspokenness, their educated, even worldly manner ("Why," said Mrs. Breen, "some of our cast speak three and four languages. Perfectly.") would impress on the Russian people a different image of the American Negro from the stereotype that continues to make Harriet Beecher Stowe one of the Soviet's best-selling authors.

Variety, the theatrical trade paper, reported as rumor a more straightforward explanation for the State Department's reversal. According to them, the International Exchange Program, a branch of the American National Theatre and Academy (ANTA), whose advice on theatrical matters carries great weight in

Washington, had registered opposition on the grounds that the State Department had already spent enough money on *Porgy and Bess,* and that the funds at their disposal should be more evenly spread to allow a larger catalogue of events in cultural exchange.

Nonetheless, ANTA and the State Department wished Everyman Opera the best of luck. They were not disowning, simply disinheriting. But well-wishers added little to Breen's bank account, and as he pondered the possibilities of raising the needed amount by private subscription, there was an unexpected development. The Russians stepped forward and offered to pick up the tab themselves. While the feeblest linguist could translate the meaning of this gesture, designed, as it was, to embarrass the State Department, American partisans of Breen's venture welcomed it for the very reason it was offered. They felt it would shame Washington into taking a less miserly position. They were mistaken.

Consequently, with time growing short, Breen had the choice of abandoning his plan or permitting the Soviet to capitalize it. A contract, dated December 3, 1955, was drawn up in Moscow between the Ministry of Culture of the U.S.S.R. ("designated hereinafter under the name of the 'Ministry' ") and Everyman Opera, Inc. ("hereinafter under the name of the 'Company' "). The contract consists of three and a half closely typed pages, and contains several quaint items—the Ministry agrees to supply a Russian mem-

ber of the cast, namely, "one domesticated she-goat."
But the burden of it is set forth in Article 5. When the
writhings of language in this long clause are disentan-
gled, it emerges that, during their stay in the Soviet
Union, the company would receive weekly payments
of $16,000, a figure quite below their customary fee,
especially so since the payments were to be made half
"in U. S. Dollars in a bank check in New York, the re-
mainder in cash Rubles at the official rate." (As
everyone knows, the official rate is an arbitrary four
rubles to the dollar. Opinion wavers on what a fair
exchange would be, but on the Moscow black market
it is possible to get ten to one, and if a person were
willing to take a chance on transporting currency out
of the country, thereby risking Siberian detention, he
could obtain in Switzerland only one dollar for every
fifteen rubles.) In addition to these monetary agree-
ments Article 5 also promised that the Ministry
would supply the Company with: "Free lodging and
food in first-class hotels or, when traveling, with
sleeper accommodations and food in a dining car. Fur-
thermore, it is understood and agreed that the Ministry pay all expenses for traveling of all members of
the Company and the transportation of its scenic
equipment to and through the Soviet Union and back
to a European border of the Soviet Union."

All told, the Russians were investing approximately $150,000. This should not be construed as cul-
tural philanthropy. Actually, for them it was a sound

business proposition. If every performance sold out, as was almost certain to happen, the Ministry would double its investment, that is, have a total box office gross the equivalent of $300,000. Whereas, on the basis of the Ministry-Company contract, and by applying the laws of income versus operating cost, it could be calculated that Everyman Opera would lose around $4,000 a week. Presumably Breen had devised a formula for sustaining such a loss. "But don't ask *me* what it is, darling," said Mrs. Gershwin. "It's an absolute mystery."

While Mrs. Breen was still on the theme of "body blows," her husband returned from the studio where he'd been rehearsing the cast after the diplomatic briefing. She asked him if he'd like a drink. He said he would, very much. Straight brandy, please.

Breen is around forty-five, a man of medium height. He has an excellent figure and one is kept aware of it by the fit of his clothes, for he is partial to trim Eisenhower jackets and those close-cut, narrow-legged trousers known as frontier pants. He wears custommade shirts, preferably in the colors black and purple. He has thinning blond hair and is seldom indoors or out without a black beret. Depending on the expression, whether solemn or smiling, his face, pale and with a smoothly gaunt bone structure, suggests altogether opposite personalities. In the solemn moments, which can last hours, his face presents a mask of brooding aloofness, as though he were posing for a

24

photographer who had warned him not to move a muscle. Inevitably, one is reminded that Breen, like his wife, has acted Shakespeare—and that the part was Hamlet, which he played in a production that, soon after the war, toured Europe and was even staged at Elsinore itself. But when Breen relaxes, or when something succeeds in catching his interest, he has a complete physical altering in the direction of extreme liveliness and boyish grinning good humor. A shyness, a vulnerable, gullible look replaces the remote and seeming self-assurance. The dual nature of Breen's appearance may explain why an Everyman Opera employee could complain in one breath, "You never know where you stand with Mr. Breen," and say in the next, "Anybody can take advantage of him. He's just too kind."

Breen took a swallow of brandy and beckoned me into the bathroom, where he wanted to demonstrate how one of the toy boats operated. It was a tin canoe with a windup Indian that paddled. "Isn't that wonderful?" he said, as the Indian paddled back and forth across the tub. "Did you ever see anything like that?" He has an actor's trained voice, "placed" in a register so very deep that it makes for automatic pomposity, and as he speaks his manicured hands move with his words, not in an excitable, Latin style, but in a gracefully slow ritualistic manner, rather as though he were saying Mass. Indeed, Breen's earliest ambitions *were* ecclesiastical. Before his interest turned toward the stage, he spent a year training to become a priest.

I asked him how the rehearsal had gone. "Well, it's a good cast," he said. "But they're a little spoiled, they take it too much for granted. Curtain calls and ovations. Rave reviews. I keep telling them, I want them to understand going to Russia isn't just another engagement. We've got to be the best we've ever been."

If Breen expected the wish contained in this last sentence to come true, then, in the estimation of some observers, he had his work cut out for him. In 1952, when Breen and his co-producer, Blevins Davis, revived the Gershwin opera, which had been a box office and somewhat of a critical failure in its original (1935) Theatre Guild presentation, the program listed William Warfield as Porgy, Leontyne Price as Bess, and Cab Calloway in the role of Sportin' Life. Since then, these stars had been replaced, and even their replacements replaced, not always with artists of comparable quality. To maintain a high level in performance is one of the chief headaches facing the proprietors of any long-run production, doubly so if the show is on tour where the strain of overnight hops, the dreamlike flow of rooms and restaurants, the electric emotional climate surrounding groups who continuously live and work together, are factors creating an accumulative fatigue that the show often reflects. Horst Kuegler, a Berlin theatre critic who, when he'd reviewed *Porgy and Bess* three years earlier (it was then appearing in Germany as part of the Berlin Music Festival), had been so enthusiastic he'd gone to see it five times, now felt, seeing it again, that it was "still full of energy and charm, though the production has deteriorated greatly." For the past week, Breen had rehearsed his cast to the limit Actors Equity permits; but whether or not the show could be whipped into prime shape, Breen had no qualms about its reception at the Leningrad premiere. It was going to be a "bombshell"! The Russians would be "stunned"! And, what was an unarguable prediction, "They'll never have seen anything like it!"

As Breen was finishing his brandy, his wife called from the next room, "You'd better get ready, Robert. They'll be here at six, and I've reserved a private dining room."

"Four Russians from the Embassy," Breen explained, showing me to the door. "They're coming over for dinner. You know, get friendly. It's friendship that counts."

When I arrived back in my own room in the Kempenski, I found waiting on my bed a large package wrapped in plain brown paper. My name was on it, the name of the hotel and the number of my room, but nothing to identify the sender. Inside, there were half a dozen thick anti-Communist pamphlets, and a handwritten card, without signature, which said, *Dear Sir*

—*You can be saved.* Saved, one presumed, from the fates described in the accompanying literature, most of which purported to be the case histories of individuals, primarily Germans, who had gone behind the iron curtain, either voluntarily or as the result of force, and had not been heard from again. It was absorbing, as only case histories can be, and I would have read through the lot uninterruptedly if the telephone hadn't rung.

The caller was Breen's secretary, Nancy Ryan. "Listen," she said, "how would you like to sleep with me? On the train, I mean. The way it works out, there are going to be four in a compartment, so I'm afraid we'll have to do as the Russians do. They always put boys and girls together. *Any*way, I'm helping assign the berths, and what with all the affections and frictions and those who want to be together and those who definitely do *not,* well, really, it's *frighten*ing. So it would simplify the situation if you and I shared a compartment with the lovebirds."

The so-called "lovebirds" were Earl Bruce Jackson, one of three alternates in the role of Sportin' Life, and Helen Thigpen, a soprano who plays the part of Serena. Jackson and Miss Thigpen had been engaged for many months. According to Everyman Opera's publicity releases, they planned to be married in Moscow.

I told Miss Ryan the arrangement sounded satisfactory. "That's brilliant," she said. "Well, see you on the train. If our visas ever come through . . ."

On Monday, the nineteenth of December, passports and visas were still in abeyance. Regardless, around three o'clock that afternoon a trio of chartered buses began circling through Berlin to collect, from the hotels and pensions where they were staying, the personnel of Everyman Opera and transport them to the railway station in East Berlin where the Soviet train, The Blue Express, was scheduled to depart at four or six or midnight, no one seemed to know for certain.

A small group, spoken of by Warner Watson as "our distinguished guests," waited together in the lobby of the Hotel Kempenski. The distinguished guests were persons who had no direct connection with *Porgy and Bess,* but had, nevertheless, been invited by the management to travel with the troupe into Russia. They amounted to: Herman Sartorius, a New York financier and close friend of Breen's; a newspaper columnist, Leonard Lyons, who was described to the Soviets in Everyman Opera's official dossier as "Company Historian," neglecting to mention that he would be mailing his history to the *New York Post;* another journalist, a Pulitzer Prize winner, Ira Wolfert, accompanied by his wife, Helen. Mr. Wolfert is on the staff of the *Reader's Digest,* and the Breens, who keep extensive scrapbooks, hoped he would do an article on their Russian adventures for that publication. Mrs. Wolfert is also an author, a poet. "A *modern* poet," she emphasized.

Mr. Lyons paced the lobby, impatient for the bus to arrive. "I'm excited. I can't sleep. Just before I left New York, Abe Burrows called me up. We live in the same building. He said you know how cold it is in Moscow? He heard on the radio it was forty below. That was day before yesterday. You got on your long underwear?" He hiked up his trouser leg to flash a stretch of red wool. Ordinarily a trim-looking man of average size, Lyons had so well prepared himself for the cold that, resplendent in a fur hat and fur-lined coat and gloves and shoes, he seemed to bulge like a shoplifter. "My wife, Sylvia, bought me three pairs of these. From Saks. They don't itch."

The financier, Herman Sartorius, attired in a conservative topcoat and business suit, as though he were setting off for Wall Street, said that no, he was not wearing long underwear. "I didn't have time to buy anything. Except a map. Did you ever try to buy a road map of Russia? Well, it's the damnedest thing. Had to turn New York upside down before I found one. Good to have on the train. Know where we are."

Lyons agreed. "But," he said, lowering his voice, and with his alert black eyes snapping from side to side, "better keep it out of sight. They might not like it. A map."

"Hmn," said Sartorius, as though he could not quite follow the drift of Lyons' thought. "Yes, well, I'll keep that in mind." Sartorius has grey hair, a height, a weight, a gentlemanly reserve that inspires the kind of confidence desirable in a financier.

"I had a letter from a friend," continued Lyons. "President Truman. He wrote me I'd better be careful in Russia because he was no longer in any position to bail me out. Russia! What a dateline!" he said, glancing around as if hunting some evidence that his elation was shared by the others.

Mrs. Wolfert said, "I'm hungry."

Her husband patted her on the shoulder. The Wolferts, who are the parents of grown children, resemble each other in that both have pink cheeks and silvering hair, a long-married, settled-down calm. "That's all right, Helen," he said, between puffs on a pipe. "Soon as we get on the train, we'll go right to the dining car."

"Sure," said Lyons. "Caviar and vodka."

Nancy Ryan came racing through the lobby, her blond hair flying, her coat flapping. "Don't stop me! There's a crisis!" She stopped, of course; and, rather as though she enjoyed imparting the bad news, said, "*Now* they tell us! Ten minutes before we leave! That there *isn't* a dining car on the train. And there *won't* be, not until we reach the Russian border. Thirty hours!"

"I'm hungry," said Mrs. Wolfert plaintively.

Miss Ryan hurried onward. "We're doing the best we can." By which she meant the management of Everyman Opera were out scouring the delicatessens of Berlin.

It was turning dark, a rain-mist was sifting through the streets when the bus arrived and, with a joking, shouting full load of passengers, rumbled off through West Berlin toward the Brandenburg Gate, where the Communist world begins.

In the bus I sat behind a couple, a young pretty member of the cast and an emaciated youth who was supposed to be a West German journalist. They had met in a Berlin jazz cellar, presumably he had fallen in love, at any rate he was now seeing her off, amid whispers and tears and soft laughter. As we neared the Brandenburg Gate, he protested that he must get off the bus. "It would be dangerous for me to go into East Berlin." Which, in retrospect, was an interesting remark. Because several weeks later who should turn up in Russia, grinning and swaggering and with no plausible explanation of how he'd got there, but this selfsame young man, still claiming to be a West German and a journalist and in love.

Beyond the Brandenburg Gate, we rode for forty minutes through the blackened acres of bombed-out East Berlin. The two additional buses, with the rest of the company, had arrived at the station before us. We joined the others on the platform where

The Blue Express waited. Mrs. Gershwin was there, supervising the loading of her luggage onto the train. She was wearing a nutria coat and, over her arm, carried a mink coat zippered into a plastic bag. "Oh, the mink's for Russia, darling. Darling," she said, "why do they call it The Blue Express? When it's not blue at all?"

It was green, a sleek collection of dark green cars hitched to a Diesel engine. The letters CCCP were painted in yellow on the side of each car, and below them, in different languages, the train's cities of destination: Berlin-Warsaw-Moscow. Soviet train officers, elegantly turned out in black Persian lamb hats and flaring princess-cut coats, were stationed at the entrances to every car. Sleeping car attendants, more humbly dressed, stood beside them. Both the officers and the attendants were smoking cigarettes in long vamp-style holders. As they watched the confusion around them, the excited milling about of the troupe, they managed to preserve a stony uninterest despite the bold attentions of those Americans who approached and stared at them as though amazed, and rather peeved, to discover Russians had two eyes correctly located.

A man from the cast walked over to one of the officers. "Tell me something, kid," he said, indicating the lettering on the side of the train, "what's that mean, CCCP?"

The Russian pointed his cigarette holder at the man. Frowning, he said, *"Sie sind Deutch?"*

The actor laughed. "I'd make a kind of funny-looking German. Seems to me I would."

A second Russian, a car attendant, spoke up. *"Sind sie nicht Deutch?"*

"Man," said the actor, "let's us settle this misery." He glanced down the platform and beckoned to Robin Joachim, a young Russian-speaking New Yorker whom Everyman Opera had hired to go along on the trip as a translator.

The two Russians smiled with pleasure when Joachim began to talk to them in their own language; pleasure gave way to astonishment as he explained that the passengers boarding their train were not Germans, but "Amerikansky" on their way to perform an opera in Leningrad and Moscow.

"Isn't that peculiar?" said Joachim, turning to a group of listeners that included Leonard Lyons. "Nobody told them a thing about us being on the train. They never heard of *Porgy and Bess.*"

Lyons, the first of the Americans to recover from the shock of this news, whipped out a notebook and pencil. "Well, what do they think? What's their reaction?"

"Oh," said Joachim, "they couldn't be happier. They're delirious with joy."

It was true that the Russians were nodding and laughing. The officer gave the attendant a hearty slap on the back and shouted an order.

"What did he say?" asked Lyons, pencil poised.

Joachim said, "He told him to go put some tea on the samovar."

A station clock said six-five. There were signs of departure, whistle sounds, a clanging of doors. In the corridors of the train a radio began blaring martial music, and the company, now all aboard, were hanging out the windows waving at dispirited German luggage porters, none of whom had received the "capitalist insult," as we'd been warned the People's Democracies consider it, of a tip. Suddenly, at every window, a cheer went up. It was for the Breens, Robert and Wilva, who were plunging along the platform, followed by a wagonload of food supplies, cardboard cases of beer and wine, frankfurters, rolls and sweet buns, cold cuts, apples and oranges. There was only time to carry the cases onto the train before the radio's military fanfare reached a crescendo, and the Breens, watching with brave parental smiles, saw their "unprecedented project" slide away from them into the night.

The space to which I'd been assigned was in Car 2, Compartment 6. It seemed larger than an ordinary wagon-lit compartment, and had a certain prettiness about it, despite the presence of a radio loud-speaker that could not be completely turned off, and a blue light bulb, burning in a blue ceiling, that could never be extinguished. The walls were blue, the window was framed with blue plush curtains which matched the seat upholstery. There was a small table between the seats, and on it a lamp with a rosy silk shade.

Miss Ryan introduced me to our companions in Compartment 6, Earl Bruce Jackson and his fiancée, Helen Thigpen, whom I'd not met before.

Jackson is tall and lean, a live-wire with slanting eyes and a saturnine face. He affects a chin goatee, and his hands are radiant with rings, diamonds and sapphires and rubies. We shook hands. "Peace, brother, peace. That's the word," he said, and resumed peeling an orange, letting the hulls drop on the floor.

"No, Earl," said Miss Ryan, "that's *not* the word. The word is, keep things tidy. Put your orange hulls in the ash tray. After all," she said, looking out the window where the lonely last lights of East Berlin were fading, "this is going to be our home for a helluva long time."

"That's right, Earl. Our home," said Miss Thigpen.

"Peace, brother, peace. That's the word. Tell the boys back in New York," said Jackson, and spit out some seed.

Miss Ryan began to distribute part of the last-minute picnic the Breens had provided. With a sigh, Miss Thigpen refused a bottle of beer and a salami sandwich. "I don't know what I'll eat. There's nothing goes with my diet. Since I met Earl, I went on a diet and lost fifty-six pounds. Five tablespoons of caviar add up to one hundred calories.''

"*This* isn't caviar. For God's sake," said Miss Ryan, her mouth full of salami sandwich.

"I'm thinking of the future," said Miss Thigpen glumly. She yawned. "Anybody object if I slip into my negligee? Might as well make ourselves comfortable.''

Miss Thigpen, a concert artist before she joined *Porgy and Bess* four years ago, is a small, plump woman, lavishly powdered. She wears the highest heels, the tallest hats, and generous sprinklings of Joy ("The World's Costliest Perfume").

"Hi there, good-lookin'," said Jackson, admiring his fiancée's efforts to make herself comfortable. "The number to play is seven seven three, and peace is the word. Ooble-ee-do!"

Miss Thigpen ignored these compliments. "Earl," she said, "it *was* São Paulo, honey?"

"Was what?"

"Was where we got engaged."

"Yeah. São Paulo. Brazil."

Miss Thigpen seemed relieved. "That's what I told Mr. Lyons. He wanted to know. He's the one writes for the paper. You met him?"

"Yeah," said Jackson. "I rubbed palms with that cat."

"Maybe you heard?" said Miss Thigpen, looking

37

at me. "About us being married in Moscow. T'was Earl's idea. I didn't even know we were engaged. I lost fifty-six pounds, but I didn't know we were engaged until Earl had this idea about us being married in Moscow."

"Bound to be a big story," said Jackson, and though he snapped his glittering fingers, his tone was serious, slow, as though thinking long thoughts. "The first couple of Negro Americans married in Moscow. That's front page. That's TV." He turned to Miss Thigpen. "And I don't want you to go telling that cat Lyons anything about it. Not till we're sure the magnetic vibrations are right. With a big thing like this, you got to feel the right vibrations."

Miss Thigpen said, "You ought to see Earl's wedding suit. He had it made in Munich."

"Crazy, man, crazy," said Jackson. "Brown tails with champagne satin lapels. Shoes to match, natch. And on top of that, I've got a brand-new overcoat with a—how d'ya call it—Persian lamb collar. But man, nobody's going to see *none* of it, not till The Day."

I asked when that would be, and Jackson admitted that no exact date had been set. "Mr. Breen's handling all the arrangements. He's talking to the Russians. It'll be a big thing for them, too."

"Sure," said Miss Ryan, retrieving orange hulls off the floor. "Put Russia on the map."

Miss Thigpen stretched out in her negligee and prepared to study a musical score; but she seemed troubled, unable to concentrate. "What bothers me, it won't be legal. Back home, in several states, they don't consider it legal, people married in Russia."

"*What* states?" said Jackson, as though resuming with her a tedious argument.

Miss Thigpen thought. "Several," she said finally.

"It's legal in Washington, D. C.," he told her. "And that's your home town. So if it's legal in your home town, what have you got to worry about?"

"Earl," said Miss Thigpen wearily, "why don't you go find your friends and have a game of Tonk?"

Tonk, popular with some elements among the cast, is a five-card variation of ordinary rummy. Jackson complained that it was useless for him to try getting up a game. "There's nowhere for us to play. All the sharps (gamblers) are bunked in with a lot of squares (non-gamblers)."

The door of our compartment was open, and Ducky James, a boyish, blond Englishman who is prop man for the production, passed by announcing, in his cockney accent, "Anybody wants a drink, we've set up a bar in our place. Martinis . . . Manhattans . . . Scotch . . ."

"That Ducky!" said Miss Thigpen. "If *he's* not the lucky one! I don't wonder he's handing out drinks. You know what happened to him? Just before we got on the train along comes this telegram. His aunt died. Leaving him ninety thousand pounds."

Jackson whistled. "How much is that in real money?"

"Two hundred and seventy thousand dollars, thereabouts," said Miss Thigpen. Then, as her future husband stood up to leave the compartment, "Where you going, Earl?"

"Just thought I'd find out if Ducky plays Tonk."

Presently we had a visit from Twerp, an all-white boxer puppy who gaily trotted into the compartment and promptly proved herself unhousebroken. She belonged to the company's wardrobe mistress, a young woman from Brooklyn named Marilyn Putnam. Miss Putnam appeared, calling, "Twerp! Twerp! Oh, *there* you are, you little bitch. Isn't she a little bitch?"

"Yes," said Miss Ryan, down on her hands and knees scrubbing at the carpet with wadded newspaper. "We have to live in here. For God's sake."

"The Russians don't mind," said Miss Putnam defensively. She scooped up her puppy and kissed its forehead. "Twerp's been being naughty up and down the corridor—haven't you, angel? The Russians just smile. *They* understand she's only a baby." She turned to leave and almost collided at the door with a girl who stood there crying. "Why, Delirious," she said to the girl, "darling, what's the matter—are you sick?"

The girl shook her head. Her chin trembled, her large eyes quivered with fresh tears.

"Delirious, honey, don't take on so," said Miss Thigpen. "Sit down. Say what's wrong."

The girl sat down. Her name was Dolores Swann; but, like many of the cast, she had acquired a nickname, in this case the descriptive Delirious. A singer in the chorus, she has red poodle-cut hair. Her pale gold face is as round as her eyes, and has the same quality of showgirl innocence. She swallowed and wailed, "I lost both my coats. Both of them. My fur coat and the blue one, too. I left them back there in the station. Not insured or anything."

Miss Thigpen clucked her tongue. "Only *you* could do a thing like that, Delirious."

"But it wasn't my fault," said Miss Swann. "I was so scared. You see, I got left behind. I missed the bus. And it was terrible, running around trying to find a taxi to take me to the station. Because none of them wanted to go to *East* Berlin. Well, finally this man spoke English and he felt sorry for me and he said he would. Well, it was terrible. Because police kept stopping us and asking questions and wanting to see papers and, oh—I was sure I was going to be left there in the pitch-black with police and Communists and whatall. I was sure I'd never see any of you again."

The reliving of her ordeal brought on more tears. Miss Ryan poured her a brandy, and Miss Thigpen squeezed her hand, saying, "It's all right, honey."

"But you can imagine how I felt, how relieved I was when I got to the station—and there everybody was. You hadn't left without me. I wanted to hug everybody. I put down my coats to hug Ducky. I hugged Ducky and forgot about my coats. Until just now.''

"Think of it like this, Delirious," said Miss Thigpen, as though searching for a comforting phrase, "just remember, you're the only person who ever went to Russia without a coat."

"I know a more unique claim that we can *all* make," said Miss Ryan. "Not only unique, but nuts. I mean, here we are—rattling off to Russia without our passports. No passports, no visa, no nothin'."

Half an hour later, Miss Ryan's claim became less valid, for when the train stopped at Frankfurt-am-Oder, which marks the German-Polish border, a delegation of officials boarded the train and, quite literally, dumped the company's long-absent passports into Warner Watson's lap.

"I don't understand it," said Watson, parading through the train delivering the passports to their individual owners. "This very morning the Russian Embassy told me the passports had gone to Moscow. Now they suddenly turn up at the Polish border."

Miss Ryan quickly rifled through her passport and found blankness on those pages where the Russian visa should have been stamped. "For God's sake, Warner. There's nothing here."

"They've issued a collective visa. They have, or they're going to, don't ask me which," said Watson,

42

his timid, tired voice skidding to a hoarse whisper. His skin was grey, and under his eyes purple bruises of fatigue were prominent as paint.

"But, Warner . . ."

Watson held up a protesting hand. "I'm not human," he said. "I've got to go to bed. I'm going to go to bed and stay there until we get to Leningrad."

"Well, it's a pity," said Miss Ryan as Watson fled, "a damned shame we can't have a stamp in our passports. I like souvenirs."

The train was scheduled to stay at the border forty minutes. I decided to get off and look around. At the end of the car, I found the exit door open and started down the small iron steps leading onto the tracks. Far ahead I could see the lights of a station, and a misty red lantern swinging back and forth. But it was dark where I was, except for the yellow squares cast by the train's windows. I walked along the tracks, liking the fresh feel of the cold and wondering whether I was in Germany or Poland. Suddenly I noticed figures running toward me, a set of shadows that, drawing nearer, turned into three soldiers, pale flat-faced men with awkward ankle-length coats and bayoneted rifles strapped to their shoulders. They stared at me in silence. Then one of them pointed to the train; he grunted and motioned for me to get back on it. We marched along together, the four of us, and I said in English that I was sorry, I hadn't realized passengers were not allowed off the train. There was no response, merely another grunt and an urging forward. I climbed the train steps and turned to wave at them. They didn't wave back.

"Darling, you haven't been *out*," said Mrs. Gershwin, whose compartment I passed in returning. "Well, you shouldn't. It isn't safe." Mrs. Gershwin was one of the two people occupying compartments to themselves. (The other was Leonard Lyons, who had obtained privacy by threatening to leave the train unless his erstwhile roommates, Herman Sartorius and Warner Watson, were removed. "It's nothing personal," he said, "but I'm a working man. I've got to turn out a thousand words a day. I can't write with a lot of characters sitting around." Sartorius and Watson had therefore been forced to move in with the Ira Wolferts. As for Mrs. Gershwin, she'd been allotted her solo status because, in the view of the management, "She deserves it. She's a Gershwin.") Without discarding her diamonds, Mrs. Gershwin had changed into slacks and a sweater; she'd tied ribbons in her hair and slippered her feet in bits of fluff. "It must have been freezing out there. I see snow on the ground. You ought to have some hot tea. Mmmmm, it's lovely," she said, sipping dark, almost black tea from a tall glass set in a silver holder with a silver handle. "That darling little man is brewing it on his samovar."

I went to look for the tea-maker, who was the attendant for Car 2; but when I found him, at the end of the corridor, he was contending with more than a blazing samovar. Twerp, the boxer puppy, was yapping between his legs and snapping at his trousers. Moreover, he was undergoing an intense interview, Lyons asking the questions and Robin Joachim acting as translator. Small and haggard, the Russian had a pushed-in, Pekingese face creased with wrinkles that seemed to indicate nutritional defects rather than age. His mouth was studded with steel teeth, and his eyelids drooped, as though he were on the verge of sleep. Between dispensing tea and fending off Twerp, he answered Lyons' quick-fire queries like a wilted housewife talking to the censor. He said he was from Smolensk. He said his feet hurt him, his back hurt him, that he always had a headache from overwork. He said he only made two hundred rubles a month ($50, but much less in actual buying power) and considered himself underpaid. He said yes, he'd very much appreciate a tip.

Lyons paused in his notetaking and said, ''I didn't know they were allowed to complain like this. The way it sounds, I get the impression this guy is a discontent.''

The attendant gave me my tea, and at the same time offered me, from a crumpled pack, one of his own cigarettes. It was two-thirds filter and one-third tobacco, good for seven or eight harsh puffs, though I didn't enjoy that many, for as I started back to my compartment the train lurched forward with an abruptness that sent both tea and cigarette flying.

Marilyn Putnam poked her head into the corridor. "Holy mackerel," she said, surveying the wreckage, "did *Twerp* do that?"

In Compartment 6 the berths had been made for the night, indeed for the whole journey, since they were never remade. Clean coarse linen, a crunchy pillow that smelled of hay, a single thin blanket. Miss Ryan and Miss Thigpen had gone to bed to read, having first turned the radio as low as it would go and opened the window a finger's width.

Miss Thigpen yawned, and asked me, "Did you see Earl, honey?"

I told her that I had. "He's teaching Ducky to play Tonk."

"Oh," said Miss Thigpen, giggling sleepily, "that means Earl won't be home till dawn."

I kicked off my shoes, and lay down in my berth, thinking in a moment I'd finish undressing. Overhead, in the berth above mine, I could hear Miss Ryan muttering to herself, as though she were reading aloud. It developed that she was studying Russian, using for the purpose an old English-Russian phrase book the U. S. Army had issued during the war for the benefit of American soldiers who might come in contact with Russians.

"Nancy," said Miss Thigpen, like a child asking for

a bedtime story, "Nancy, say us something in Russian."

"The only thing I've learned is *Awr-ga-nih-ya ra-neen . . .*" Miss Ryan faltered. She took a deep breath. ". . . *V-pa-lavih-yee*. Wow! I only wanted to learn the alphabet. So I can read street signs."

"But that was nice, Nancy. What does it mean?"

"It means, 'I have been wounded in the privates.' "

"Really, Nancy," said Miss Thigpen, bewildered, "why on earth would you care to memorize something like that?"

"Go to sleep," said Miss Ryan, turning off her reading light.

Miss Thigpen yawned again. She pulled the covers up to her chin. "I'm about ready to."

Soon, lying there, I had a sense of stillness traveling through the train, seeping through the cars like the wintry color of the blue light bulb. Frost was spreading at the corners of the window; it seemed like a web-weaving in reverse. On the muted radio an orchestra of balalaikas made shivery music; like an odd and lonely counterpoint, someone somewhere nearby was playing a harmonica.

"Listen," whispered Miss Thigpen, calling attention to the harmonica. "That's Junior," she said, meaning Junior Mignatt, a member of the cast still in his teens. "Don't you know that boy is lonesome? He's from Panama. He's never seen snow before."

"Go to sleep," said Miss Ryan. The northern roar

of wind at the window seemed to echo her command. The train shrieked into a tunnel. For me, fallen asleep fully clothed, the tunnel lasted all night long.

Coldness woke me. Snow was blowing through the window's minute opening. Enough had settled at the foot of my berth to scoop into a snowball. I got up, glad I'd gone to bed with my clothes on, and closed the window. It was blurred with ice. I rubbed a part of it until I could peer out. There were hints of sunrise on the rim of the sky, yet it was still dark, and the traces of morning color were like goldfish swimming in ink. We were on the outskirts of a city. Rural lamplighted houses gave way to cement blocks of forlorn, look-alike apartment dwellings. The train rumbled over a bridge that spanned a street; below, a frail streetcar, jammed with people on their way to work, careened round a curve like a rickety bobsled. Moments later we pulled into a station, which by now I realized must be Warsaw. On a dim, snow-deep platform gangs of men stood clustered together stamping their feet and slapping their ears. I noticed our car attendant, the tea-maker, join one of the groups. He gestured toward the train and said something that made them laugh. An explosion of breath-smoke filled the air. Still laughing, several of the men approached the train. I slipped back into bed, for it was obvious that they intended to peek in the windows. One after another, distorted faces mashed themselves against the glass. Presently I heard a short scream. It came from a compartment further ahead and sounded like Dolores Swann. Screams were understandable if she'd wakened to see, looming at the window, one of these frosty masks. Though it roused none of my own companions, I waited, expecting a commotion in the car, but quietness resumed, except for Twerp, who started barking with a regular rhythm that sent me off to sleep again.

At ten, when I opened my eyes, we were in a wild, crystal world of frozen rivers and snowfields. Here and there, like printing on paper, stretches of fir trees interrupted the whiteness. Flights of crows seemed to skate on a sky hard and shiny as ice.

"Man," said Earl Bruce Jackson, just awake and sleepily scratching himself as he stared out the window, "I'm telling you. They don't grow oranges here."

The washroom in Car 2 was a bleak unheated chamber. There was a rusty washbasin with the customary two faucets, hot and cold. Unfortunately, they both leaked a frigid trickle. That first morning a long queue of men waited at the washroom door, toothbrushes in one hand, shaving tackle in the other. Ducky James had the notion of asking the attendant, who was busily stoking the little coal fire under his samovar, to part with some of his tea water and "gives us blokes a chance at a decent shave." Everyone thought this a splendid idea except the Russian, for when the request was translated to him he looked at his samovar as though it were bubbling with melted diamonds. Then he did a curious thing.

He stepped up to each man and brushed his finger-tips against their cheeks, examining their beard stubble. There was a tenderness in the action that made it memorable. "Boy," said Ducky James, "he sure is affectionate."

But the attendant concluded his researches with a headshake. Absolutely no, *nyet,* he would not give away his hot water. The condition of the gentlemen's beards did not justify such a sacrifice, and besides, when traveling, the "realistic" man should expect to go unshaven. "My water is for tea," he said. "Hot and sweet and good for the spirit."

A steaming glass of it went with me into the washroom. I used it for brushing my teeth, and then, combining it with soap, transformed it into a shaving cream. Rather sticky, but not bad at all.

Afterwards, feeling spruce, I commenced a round of visits. The occupant of Compartment 1, Leonard Lyons, was having a professional tête-à-tête with Earl Bruce Jackson. Clearly Jackson had overcome his fear that Lyons might not possess the "right vibrations," for he was describing to him the details of his forthcoming Moscow marriage.

"That's great. Just great, Earl," said Lyons,

scribbling away. "Brown tails. Champagne satin lapels. Now—who's going to be your best man?"

Jackson told him he'd invited Warner Watson to serve in that capacity. Lyons seemed reluctant to approve the choice. "Listen," he said, tapping Jackson on the knee, "did you ever think of asking somebody, well, important?"

"Like you, you mean?"

"Like *Khrushchev*," said Lyons. "Like *Bulganin*."

Jackson's eyes narrowed, as though he couldn't decide whether Lyons' suggestion was serious or a leg pull. "But I already ask Warner. But maybe, under that kind of circumstance . . ."

"Sure," said Lyons, "Warner would understand."

Still, Jackson had one last vestige of doubt. "You think Mr. Breen can arrange it, to get me one of those cats?"

"He could try," said Lyons. "And just trying, see, that could land you on the front page."

"*C'est* ooble-ee-do," said Jackson, gazing at Lyons with perfect admiration. "Really crazy, man. Gone."

Further along the corridor, I called on the Wolferts, who were sharing their compartment with Herman Sartorius and Warner Watson, the pair Lyons had evicted, the latter in more ways than one. But Watson was still asleep, unaware of his impending dismissal as Jackson's best man. Sartorius and Ira Wolfert were sitting with an immense map spread across their collective lap, and Mrs. Wolfert, bundled in a fur coat, was hunched over a manuscript. I asked if she were keeping a journal.

"I *do*. Only this is a poem. I've been working on it since last January. I thought I might finish it on the train. But the way I feel . . ." she said dismally. "I didn't sleep a wink last night. My hands are cold. My head's whirling with impressions. I don't know where I am."

Sartorius placed a fastidious finger on his map. "I'll tell you where we are. We've passed Liedce. Now we've got about five more hours of Poland before Brest Litovsk."

Brest Litovsk was to be the first stop in Russia. A good deal was scheduled to happen there. The wheels of the train would be changed to fit Russia's wide-gauge tracks; a dining car would be attached, and, most importantly, representatives from the Ministry of Culture were to meet the company and travel on with them to Leningrad.

"Know what this reminds me of," said Ira Wolfert, pointing a pipe at the severe landscape. "Parts of America. The West."

Sartorius nodded. "Wyoming in the winter."

Returning to the corridor, I encountered Miss Ryan, still wearing her bed costume, a red flannel night-shirt. She was hopping on one foot, her other foot

having made contact with a sample of Twerp's misbe-
havior.

I said, "Good morning."

She said, *"Don't speak to me,"* and hopped away
toward the washroom.

Next, I went to Car 3, where the family groups,
children and their parents, were installed. School had
just let out; that is, the children had finished their
morning lessons and were consequently in sportive
spirit. Paper planes sailed through the air. Carica-
tures were being finger-drawn on the frosted windows.
The Russian attendant, who looked even more mourn-
ful and harassed than his colleague in Car 2, was kept
at such a hop protecting Soviet property that he
hadn't noticed what was happening to his samovar.
Two little boys had taken it over and were roasting
hot dogs. One of them, Davy Bey, offered me a bite.
"Good, huh?" I told him it was indeed. Well, he said,
if I liked it that much, then I could have the rest of it;
he'd already eaten fifteen.

"You see the wolves?" he asked.

An older friend, Gail Barnes, told him, "Stop making stories, Davy. They weren't wolves. They were
plain dogs."

"Was wolves," said Davy, who has a snub nose and
a wicked tilt to his eyes. "Everybody saw them. Out
the window. They *looked* like dogs. Police dogs, only
littler. And what they were up to, they were chasing

each other round and round in the snow. Like they were having a grand time. I coulda killed one dead. Woooooolves," he howled, and poked me in the stomach with a cowboy pistol.

Gail said that she hoped I understood. "Davy's only a child." Gail, whose father, Irving Barnes, alternates in the role of Porgy, is eleven, the oldest of the company's six children, most of whom play minor parts in the show. Because of her seniority, she has developed a sense of big-sister responsibility toward all the children, and handles them with mature good nature, a firm politeness that could set any governess an example. "Excuse me," she said, glancing down the corridor where several of her charges, by managing to open a window, were letting in blasts of Arctic wind. "I'm afraid I'll have to put a stop to that."

But before she had completed her mission, Gail herself was swept away into being a child again. "Oh, look," she cried, hanging out the very window she'd gone to close. "Look, kids . . . *People!*"

The people were two small children ice-skating on a long ribbon of pond at the edge of a white wood. They skated fast as they could, trying to keep up with the train, and as it sped beyond them they stretched out their arms, as though to catch the shouted greetings, the blown kisses of Gail and her friends.

Meanwhile, the Russian attendant had discovered smoke billowing from his samovar. He snatched charred hot dogs off the fire, and tossed them on the floor. Then, sucking blistered fingers and employing a vocabulary that must have been, to judge from its tone, on the blistery side itself, he rushed to pry the children away from the window and slam it shut.

"Aw, don't be a sorehead," Davy told him. "We're just having a grand time."

The remnants of a cheese and fruit lunch were scattered on the table (and the carpet) of Compartment 6. Midafternoon sunlight sparkled in a glass of Chianti Miss Ryan was revolving in her hand. "I adore wine," she said fervently. "I began drinking it when I was twelve. Heavily. It's a wonder I'm not a wino." She sipped and sighed with a contentment that reflected the general mood. Miss Thigpen and her fiancé, who'd had their share of Chianti, were nestled together in a corner of their seat, her head resting on his shoulder. The drowsy, dreaming spell was broken by a knock at the door, and someone saying, "This is it. Russia."

"Places, please," said Miss Ryan. "Curtain going up."

The first signs of an approaching frontier came into view: stark wooden guard towers, not unsimilar to those that encircle Southern convict farms. Spread at wide intervals, they marched across the wastes like giant telephone poles. In the nearest of them I could see a man watching the train through binoculars. The train slowed round a curve and slackened to a stop.

We were in a switch yard, surrounded by a maze of tracks and halted freight cars. It was the Soviet border, forty minutes from Brest Litovsk.

Along the tracks, herds of women with shawl-wrapped heads, like a wooly version of purdah, were swinging picks, shoveling snow, pausing only to blow their noses into naked, raw-red hands. The few who even glanced at The Blue Express risked sharp looks from various militia men lounging about with their hands stuffed in their coat pockets.

"If that's not a *shame*," said Miss Thigpen. "Ladies doing all the work, while the men just stand around. How disgraceful!"

"That's what it is here, honey," said Jackson, puffing on one of his ruby rings, and polishing it against his lapel. "Every man a Sportin' Life."

"I'd like to see somebody treat *me* that way," replied Miss Thigpen, warningly.

"But I must say," said Miss Ryan, "the men are pretty divine." Her interest was fixed on a pair of officers pacing below the window, tall-strong-silent types with thin lips and rugged, windburned faces. One of them looked up and, catching sight of Miss Ryan's blue eyes and long golden hair, lost step with his partner. Miss Ryan whimpered, "Oh, wouldn't it be awful!"

"Awful what, honey?" said Miss Thigpen.

"If I fell in love with a Russian," said Miss Ryan. "Wouldn't that be the absolute *fin*? Actually, my mother's afraid that I might. She said if I fell in love with any Russians I needn't bother coming home. But," she added, her gaze again drifting toward the officer, "if they're all like *that* . . ."

Quite suddenly Miss Ryan's admirer had no time for flirtation. He became part of a small Russian army chasing round the yard after Robin Joachim. Joachim, an overly avid photographer, had broken the rules by getting off the train, then compounded that error by attempting to take pictures. Now he was racing zigzag across the tracks, narrowly avoiding the wrathful swipe of a woman worker's shovel, barely eluding the grasp of a guard.

"I hope they catch him," said Miss Ryan coldly. "Him and his goddam cameras. I knew he'd get us into trouble."

Joachim, however, turned out to be a resourceful young man. Slipping past his pursuers, he hurled himself onto the train, rushed into a compartment, threw his coat, his camera and cap under the seat, and to further alter his appearance, whipped off his horn-rimmed glasses. Seconds later, when the angry Soviets came aboard, he calmly assumed his role of company translator and helped them hunt the culprit, a search that included every compartment. Warner Watson, roused from his slumbers, was the person least amused by the situation. He promised Joachim a good talking to. "This," he said, "is *not* the way to begin a cultural exchange."

The incident caused the train to be delayed forty-five minutes and had other repercussions as well, one of them involving Twerp, for the Russians, in the course of their search, had been appalled by certain conditions in Car 2 attributable to the puppy. Twerp's owner, Marilyn Putnam, said later, "I put it to them straight. I said, since we're never allowed off the train, what the hell do you expect? That shut 'em up."

We reached Brest Litovsk in a luminous twilight. Statues of political heroes, painted cheap-silver like those souvenir figures sold at Woolworth's, saluted us along the last mile of track leading to the station. The station was on high ground that afforded a partial view of the city, dim and blue and dominated, far-off, by an Orthodox cathedral, whose onion-domes and mosaic towers still projected, despite the failing light, their Oriental colors.

Among the company it had been rumored that we would be allowed off the train here, and perhaps, while the wheels were changed and the dining car added, permitted to tour the city. Leonard Lyons was most anxious that this should happen. "I can't write a thousand words a day just sitting on a train. I need action." Lyons had gone so far as to discuss with the cast the kind of action he would like. He wanted them to traipse around Brest Litovsk singing spirituals. "It's a good story and it's good showmanship. I'm surprised Breen didn't think of it." When the train stopped, the doors opened all right, but were immediately closed again, after admitting a five-man delegation from Moscow's Ministry of Culture.

One of these emissaries was a middle-aged woman with straying dishwater hair and, except for her eyes, what seemed a kind, motherly face. The eyes, dull grey and flecked with dots of milky white, had an embalmed glaze that did not blend with the cheerful contours of her expression. She wore a black cloth coat and a rusty black dress that sagged at the breasts from the weight of an ivory rose. In introducing herself and her colleagues, she ran the names together so that it sounded like a patter song. "You will please to meet Sascha Menasha Tiomken Kerinsky Ivors Ivanovich Nikolai Savchenko Plesitskya Grutchenko Ricki Somanenko . . ."

In due time, the Americans were to sort and simplify these names until their owners became familiar as Miss Lydia, Henry, Sascha and Igor, the latter young underlings from the Ministry who, like the middle-aged Miss Lydia, had been assigned to the company as translators. But the fifth member of the quintet, Nikolai Savchenko, was not the man you call Nick. An important official in the Ministry, Savchenko was in charge of the *Porgy and Bess* tour.

The victim of a slightly receding chin, mildly bulging eyes and a tendency toward fat, he was nevertheless a formidable figure—well over six feet, with a stern, no-nonsense attitude and a handshake like a nutcracker. Beside him, his young assistants looked like sickly children, though two of them, Sascha and Igor, were strapping boys whose shoulders were too broad for their fur-collared coats; and Henry, a spidery mite with huge ears so red they were purple, made up by personal vividness what he lacked in stature.

It seemed natural that Miss Lydia and the young men should react awkwardly to this, their first encounter with Westerners; understandable that they should hesitate to test their English, so tediously learned at Moscow's Institute of Foreign Languages but never before practiced on bona fide foreigners; forgivable that they should, instead, stare as though the Americans represented pawns in a chess problem. But Savchenko also gave an impression of being ill at ease, of preferring, in fact, a stretch in Lubyanka to his present chores. Which was excusable, too; though rather odd when you consider that for two years during the war he served as Counsel at the Soviet Embassy in Washington. Even so, he seemed to find Americans such a tongue-tying novelty that for the moment he affected not to speak English. He delivered a small speech of welcome in gruff Russian, then had it translated by Miss Lydia. "We hope each and all have had a pleasant journey. Too bad you see us in the winter. It is not the good time of year. But we have the saying, Better now than never. Your visit is a step forward in the march toward peace. When the cannons are heard, the muses are silent; when the cannons are silent, the muses are heard."

The muse-cannon metaphor, which was to prove a Savchenko favorite, the starring sentence of all future speeches, was an instant hit with his listeners ("A beautiful thing." "Just great, Mr. Savchenko." "That's cool cookin', man."), and Savchenko, warmed by success and beginning to relax, decided there was perhaps no reason to keep the company cooped up in the train. Why not step out on the platform and watch the changing of the wheels?

Outside, Lyons canvassed the group, trying to work up a song fest. But the temperature, ten below zero, was not conducive to a musical mood. Moreover, a large percentage of those who had been grateful to escape The Blue Express were, after the briefest exposure, shoving each other to get back in. The hearties who remained watched in the nightfall as workers of both sexes uncoupled the cars and jacked them to the height of a man. The old wheels, spraying sparks, were then rolled from under the train, while from the opposite direction the new wide-gauge wheels came gliding into place. Ira Wolfert called the operation "very efficient"; Herman Sartorius considered it "most impressive"; but Miss Ryan thought it was a "damned bore" and said that if I'd follow her into the station, she would buy me a vodka.

No one stopped us. We crossed a hundred yards of track, walked down a dirt lane between warehouses, and arrived at what appeared to be a combination of a parking lot and a market place. Brightly lighted kiosks circled it like candles burning on a cake. It was puzzling to discover that each of the kiosks sold the same products: cans of Red Star salmon, Red Star sardines, dusty bottles of Kremlin perfume, dusty boxes of Kremlin candy, pickled tomatoes, hairy slabs of raw bacon slapped between thick slices of grime-colored bread, weird liqueurs, cross buns (without the cross) that one somehow felt had been baked last July. And though the kiosks were attracting a brisk trade, the most sought-after item was not on sale at any of them. It was in the private hands of a peddler, an elderly Chinese who carried a tray of apples. The apples were as shriveled and miniature as himself, but his waiting line of customers appeared disconsolate when the last of them evaporated. At the far end of the area a flight of steps led to the main entrance of the station, and the Chinese, folding his empty tray, wandered over to them and sat down next to a friend. The friend was a beggar bundled in an old army coat and with a pair of crutches sprawled beside him like the wings of a wounded bird. Every third or fourth person going by dropped a coin into his hand. The Chinese gave him something, too. An apple. He'd saved one for the beggar, and one for himself. The two friends gnawed their apples and leaned against each other in the cutting cold.

The constant wailing of a train whistle seemed to fuse the apple-eaters and the kiosks and the batlike passings of fur-shrouded faces into a smoky, single image of its woeful sound. "I've never been homesick. Never in my life," Miss Ryan informed me. "But sometimes, for God's sake. Sometimes," she said, running up the steps and pushing open the doors of the station, "you do feel a long *way* from home."

Since Brest Litovsk is one of Russia's most strategic railroad centers, its station is among the country's largest. Looking for somewhere to buy a drink, we explored lofty corridors and a series of waiting rooms, the principal one furnished with handsome oak benches occupied by many passengers with very few suitcases. Children and paper bundles filled their laps. The stone floors, soggy with black slush, made slippery walking, and there was an odor in the air, a saturation so heavy it seemed less a smell than a pressure. Travelers to Venice often remark on the vivid scents of that city. The public places of Russia, terminals and department stores, restaurants and theatres, also have a reek instantly recognizable. And Miss Ryan, taking her first sniff of it, said, "Boy, I wouldn't want a bottle of this. Old socks and a million yawns."

In the search for a bar, we began opening doors at random. Miss Ryan sailed through one and out again. It was a men's room. Then, spotting a pair of dead-drunks as they emerged from behind a small red door, she decided, "That's the place we're looking for." The red door led into an extraordinary restaurant. The size

of a gymnasium, it looked as if it had been done over
for a school prom by a decorating committee with
Victorian tastes. Plush crimson draperies were looped
along the walls. Other-era chandeliers distributed a
tropic glare that beat down on a jungle of borscht-
stained tablecloths and withering rubber plants. The
maître d'hôtel seemed appropriate to this atmosphere
of grandeur gone to seed. He was at least eighty years
old, a white-bearded patriarch with ferocious eyes that
peered at us, through a sailor's-dive haze of cigarette
smoke, as though questioning our right to be there.

Miss Ryan smiled at him and said, "Vodka, *pjo-
lista.*" The old man stared at her with more hostility
then comprehension. She tried varying pronuncia-
tions, "Woedka . . . Wadka . . . Woodka," and even
performed a bottoms-up pantomime. "The poor
thing's deaf," she said, and shouted, "*Vodka.* For
God's sake."

Although his expression remained unenlightened,
the old man beckoned us forward and, following the
Russian custom of seating strangers together, put us
at a table with two men. They both were drinking beer,
and the old man pointed at it, as if asking, was this
what we wanted? Miss Ryan, resigning herself, nodded.

Our companions at the table were two very different
specimens. One, a beefy boy with a shaved head and
wearing some sort of faded uniform, was well on his
way to being drunk, a condition shared by a surpris-
ing lot of the restaurant's clientele, most of whom

were male, many of them either boisterous or slumped across their tables mumbling to themselves. The second man was an enigma. In appearance he might have been a Wall Street partner of Herman Sartorius, the kind of person better imagined dining at the Pavillon than sipping beer in Brest Litovsk. His suit was pressed, and one could see that he hadn't sewn it himself. There were gold cuff links in his shirt, and he was the only man in the room sporting a tie.

After a moment the shaven-headed soldier spoke to Miss Ryan. "I'm afraid I don't speak Russian," she told him. "We're Americans. *Amerikansky.*" Her declaration had a somewhat sobering effect. His reddened eyes slowly came into semifocus. He turned to the well-dressed man and made a long statement, at the end of which the man answered him with several chiseled, cold-sounding sentences. There followed between them a sharp repartee, then the soldier took his beer and stalked to another table, where he sat glowering. "Well," said Miss Ryan, glowering back, "not *all* the men are attractive, that's for sure." However, she considered our apparent defender, the well-dressed man: "Very attractive. Sort of Otto Kruger. Funny, I've always liked older men. Stop staring. He'll know we're talking about him. Listen," she said, after calling attention to his shirt, his cuff links, his clean fingernails, "do you suppose there's such a thing as a Russian millionaire?"

The beer arrived. A quart bottle and two glasses.

The maître d'hôtel poured an inch of beer into my glass, then waited expectantly. Miss Ryan saw the point before I did. "He wants you to *taste* it, like wine." Lifting the glass, I wondered if beer-tasting was a Soviet commonplace, or if it was a ceremony, some confused champagne-memory of Czarist elegance that the old man had revived to impress us. I sipped, nodded, and the old man proudly filled our glasses with a warm and foamless brew. But Miss Ryan said suddenly, "Don't touch it. It's dreadful!" I told her I didn't think it was that bad. "I mean, we're in dreadful trouble," she said. "I mean, my God, we can't pay for this. I completely forgot. We haven't any rubles."

"Please, won't you be my guests?" inquired a soft voice in beautifully accented English. It was the well-dressed man who had spoken, and though his face was perfectly straight, his eyes, a bright Nordic blue, wrinkled with an amusement that took full measure of our discomfort. "I am not a Russian millionaire. They *do* exist—I know quite a few—but it would give me pleasure to pay for your drink. No, please, there is no cause to apologize," he said, in response to Miss Ryan's stammered efforts, and openly smiling, "it's been the keenest enjoyment. Very unusual. Very unusual to run across Americans in this part of the world. Are you Communists?"

After disabusing him of that notion, Miss Ryan told him where we were going, and why. "You are fortunate that you go to Leningrad first. A lovely city," he said, "very quiet, really European, the one place in Russia I could imagine living, not that I do, but still . . . Yes, I like Leningrad. It's not the least like Moscow. I'm on my way to Warsaw, but I've just been two weeks in Moscow. That's equal to two months anywhere else." He told us that he was Norwegian, and that his business, lumber, had required him to visit the Soviet Union several weeks of every year, except for a gap during the war, since 1931. "I speak the language quite well, and among my friends I don't mind passing as a Russian authority. But to be honest, I can't say I understand much more about it now than I did in 1931. Whenever I go to your country—I've been there, oh, I guess a half dozen times—it always strikes me that Americans are the only people who remind me of Russians. You don't object to my saying that? Americans are so generous. Energetic. And underneath all that brag they have such a wishing to be loved, they want to be petted, like dogs and children, and told that they are just as good and even better than the rest of us. Well, Europeans are inclined to agree with them. But they simply won't believe it. They go right on feeling inferior and far away. Alone. Like Russians. Precisely."

Miss Ryan wanted to know the substance of his dialogue with the soldier who had left the table. "Oh, silly rot," he said. "Alcoholic bravado. For some foozled reason he thought you had insulted him. I told him he was being *nye kulturni.* Remember that: *nye kulturni.* You'll find it extremely useful, because when these chaps are rude and you feel obliged to tick them off, it means not a whit to call them a bastard, a son of a dog, but to tell him he's *uncultured,* that really strikes home."

Miss Ryan was growing anxious about the time. We shook hands with the gentleman and thanked him for the beer. "You've been very *kulturni,*" she said. "And by the way, I think you're *more* attractive than Otto Kruger."

"I shall certainly tell my wife," he said grinning. "*Dazvedanya.* Good luck."

An hour out of Brest Litovsk, the first call to the dining car was announced. It was an event the company had looked forward to with appetites excited by both genuine hunger and the conviction that the Soviet hosts were bound to make this, the company's first Russian meal, a "real spread"; or, as another of the cast forthrightly phrased it, "a bust-gut."

Miss Thigpen's desires were the most modest. "Five spoons of caviar and a piece of dry toast. That's one hundred and thirty calories." Calories were Mrs. Gershwin's last concern. "Don't think I'm not going to tear into the cavy, darling. It cost thirty-five dollars a pound in Beverly Hills." The dreams of Leonard Lyons centered around hot borscht and sour cream. Earl Bruce Jackson planned to "stone" himself with vodka and "slay" himself with shashlik.

Marilyn Putnam hoped that everyone would save little tidbits for Twerp.

The first sitting, fifty strong, marched into the dining car and took their places at linen-covered tables, each seating four, that ran down either side of the aisle. The tables were set with white crockery and smoothly worn silver. The diner itself seemed as old as the silver, and the smell of cooking, a half-century's worth, hung in the air like a visible steam. Savchenko was absent, but Miss Lydia and the three young men from the Ministry played host at different tables. The young men kept gazing round, as though silently calling to each other from separate islands of exile and misery.

Miss Lydia shared a table with Lyons, Miss Ryan and myself. One sensed that for this middle-aged woman, who said that her ordinary life was translating articles and living in a room in Moscow, the unique experience, the one that brought such a flush to her cheeks, was not that she was talking to foreigners, but that she was sitting in a dining car riding on a train. Something about the silver and the clean cloth and a little basket of puckered apples, like those the Chinese man had sold, made her fuss with her ivory rose and tuck up the straying ends of her hair. "Ah, we eat!" she said, her eyes shifting toward a quartet of chunky waitresses who came waddling down the aisle with trayloads of the first course.

Those whose palates had been anticipating iced cav-

iar and chilled carafes of vodka were a bit chagrined
to see, set before them, yogurt accompanied by bottles
of raspberry soda. Miss Thigpen, seated behind me,
was the sole voice expressing enthusiasm: "I just
could kiss them! More proteins than a steak and only
half the calories." But across the aisle, Mrs. Gershwin
warned Miss Putnam not to ruin her appetite by eat-
ing it. "Don't, darling, I'm sure the cavy will come
along next." The next course, however, consisted of
stiff noodles lying like sunken logs in a watery broth.
The entree that followed featured breaded veal cutlets,
boiled potatoes, and peas that rattled on the plate like
gunshot; to wash this down, there were further provi-
sions of raspberry soda. Miss Putnam said to Mrs.
Gershwin, "It's not *my* stomach I'm worried about.
It's Twerp's," and Mrs. Gershwin, sawing at her
cutlet, said, "Do you suppose they could be saving the
cavy for dessert? You know, with little pancakes?"

Miss Lydia's cheeks bulged, her eyes popped, her
jaws pumped like pistons, a trickle of sweat ran down
her neck. "Eat, eat," she urged, "it's good, yes?"
Miss Ryan told her it was wonderful, and Miss Lydia,
swabbing her plate with a quarter loaf of black bread,
nodded vehemently: "You will not obtain better in
Moscow itself."

During the lull between entree and dessert, she went
to work on the basket of apples; as the cores piled up
she paused occasionally to answer questions. Lyons
was anxious to learn at what hotel the company would

be staying in Leningrad. Miss Lydia was startled that he didn't know. "The Astoria. For weeks the rooms have been reserved," she said, and went on to describe the Astoria as "very old-fashion but exquisite." "Well," said Lyons, "what about the night life in Leningrad, any action there?" Miss Lydia replied by saying that perhaps her English was not all it should be, and proceeded, from her Muscovite point of view, to discuss Leningrad rather as a New Yorker might Philadelphia; it was "old-fashion," it was "provincial," it was "not the same like Moscow." At the end of this recital, Lyons said glumly, "Sounds like a two-day town to me." Miss Ryan thought to ask, when was the last time Miss Lydia had visited Leningrad? Miss Lydia blinked. "The last time? Never. I have never been there. It will be interesting to see, yes?"

Presently she had a question of her own. "I would appreciate you to explain to me. Why is Paul Robeson not in with the players? *He* is a colored person, yes?"

"Yes," said Miss Ryan; and so, she added, were sixteen million other Americans. Surely Miss Lydia didn't expect *Porgy and Bess* to employ them all?

Miss Lydia leaned back in her chair with a cunning, I'm-no-fool expression. "It is because *you*," she said, smiling at Miss Ryan, "*you* do not permit him his passport."

The dessert arrived. It was vanilla ice cream, and it was excellent. Behind me, Miss Thigpen said to her fiancé, "Earl, honey, I wouldn't touch it. Maybe it's

71

not pasteurized." Across the aisle, Mrs. Gershwin observed to Miss Putnam, "It's my theory they send it all to California. It cost thirty-five dollars a pound in Beverly Hills."

Coffee followed, and with it an altercation. Jackson and several of his friends had taken over a table and were dealing out a game of Tonk. The two huskiest of the Ministry's young men, Sascha and Igor, converged on the card players and informed them, their voices struggling to sound firm, that "gambling" was illegal in the Soviet Union. "Man," said one of the players, "nobody's gambling here. We got to do *something*. We don't have a friendly game, we blow our stacks." Sascha insisted, "It's illegal. Not allowed." The men threw down their cards, and Jackson, tucking them into a case, said, "Old Squareville. Home for dead cats. The number to play is zero. Tell the boys back in New York."

"They are unhappy. We regret," said Miss Lydia. "But we must remember our restaurant workers." Her stubby-fingered hand motioned elegantly toward the waitresses, whose blear-eyed, solid faces glistened with perspiration as they shambled down the aisle balancing a hundred pounds of dirty dishes. "You understand. It would not look well for them to see the laws disenforced." She gathered the last few apples, and stuffed them into a cloth handbag. "Now," she said cheerfully, "we go to dream. We unravel the sleeve of care."

On the morning of December 21, The Blue Express was twenty-four hours from Leningrad, another day and night, though the difference between the two seemed, as the train crawled deeper into Russia, tenuous indeed, so little did the sun, a grey ghost rising at ten and returned to its grave by three, help to divide them. The fragile span of daylight continued to reveal winter at its uncrackable hardest: birches, their branches broken from the weight of snow; a log-cabin village, not a soul in sight and the roofs hung with icicles heavy as elephant tusks. Once, a village cemetery, poor plain wooden crosses, wind-bent and all but buried. But here and there haystacks, standing in deserted fields, were evidence that even this harsh ground could, in distant spring, grow green again.

Aboard, among the passengers, the emotional pendulum had settled at that nirvana point between the strains of departure and the tensions of arrival. An on and on timeless nowhere that one accepted as perhaps lasting forever, like the wind that swept white cauldrons of snow-spray against the train. At last, even Warner Watson relaxed. "Well," he said, lighting a cigarette with hands that scarcely trembled, "I guess maybe I've got my nerves fenced in." Twerp snoozed in the corridor, pink stomach upturned, paws awry. In Compartment 6, by now a welter of unmade berths, orange peelings, spilled face powder and cigarette butts floating in cold tea, Jackson practiced card-shuffling while his fiancée buffed her nails, and Miss

Ryan, pursuing her Russian studies, memorized a new phrase out of the old army textbook; "sloo-*sha eess-ya ee-lee ya* boo-*doo streel*-yaht! Obey or I'll fire!" Lyons alone stayed faithful to the pressures of a workaday world. "Nobody gets in my tax bracket looking at scenery," he said, sternly typing the heading for a new column: *"Showtrain to Leningrad."*

At seven that evening, when the others had gone off to the day's third round of yogurt and raspberry soda, I stayed in the compartment and dined on a Hershey chocolate bar. I thought Twerp and I had the car to ourselves until I noticed one of the Ministry's interpreters, Henry, the child-sized young man with the large ears, pass my door, then pass again, each time giving me a glance that quivered with curiosity. It was as though he wanted to speak but caution and timidity prevented him. When finally, after another reconnoiter, he did come into the compartment, the approach he'd designed was official.

"Give me your passport," he said, with that bluntness shy people often assume.

He sat on Miss Thigpen's berth, and studied the passport through a pair of spectacles that kept sliding to the tip of his nose; like everything he wore, from his shiny black suit with its bell-bottom trousers to his brown worn-down shoes, they were much too big for him. I said if he would tell me what he was looking for, possibly I could help him. "It is necessary," he mumbled, his red ears burning like hot coals. The train must have traveled several miles while he fingered through the passport like a boy poring over a stamp album; and though he carefully examined the mementos left on its pages by immigration authorities, his attention lingered longest on the data that states one's occupation, height and color, date of birth.

"Here is correct?" he said, pointing to my birth date. I told him it was. "We are three years apart," he said. "I am youngest—*younger?*—I am younger, thank you. But you have seen much. So. I have seen Moscow." I asked him if he would like to travel. His answer began as a physical action, a queer sequence of shrugs and flutterings, shrinking inside his fat man's suit that seemed to mean yes and no, perhaps. He pushed up his spectacles, and said, "I have not the time. I am a worker like him and him. Three years, it could also happen my passport has many imprimaturs. But I am content with the scenic—no, *scenery*—scenery of the mind. The world is the same, but here," he tapped his forehead, struck it really, *"here,"* he spread a hand over his heart, "are changefuls. Which is correct; chang*ings* or change*fuls?*" I said either one; as used, they both made sense.

The effort of shaping these sentences, and an excess of feeling behind them, had left him breathless. He leaned on his elbow and rested a spell before suddenly observing, "You resemble Shostakovich. That is cor-

rect?" I told him I wouldn't have thought so, not
from the photographs of Shostakovich that I'd seen.
"We have discuss it. Mr. Savchenko has also the opinion," he said, as though this were final, for who were
we, either of us, to challenge Savchenko? Shostakovich's name led to mention of David Oistrakh, the
great Soviet violinist who had recently played concerts in New York and Philadelphia. He listened to
my report of Oistrakh's American triumphs as if I
were praising him, Henry; his hunched shoulders
straightened, all at once he seemed to fill out his flapping suit, and the heels of his shoes, dangling over the
side of the berth, swung together and clicked, clicked
and swung, as though he were dancing a jig. I asked
him if he thought *Porgy and Bess* would have a success in Russia comparable to Oistrakh's American reception. "It is not my ability to say. But we at the
Ministry hope more than you hope. A real man's job
for us, that *Porgy-Bess.*" He told me that although
he'd worked at the Ministry for five years, this was
the only time his job had taken him outside Moscow.
Usually, he said, he spent six days a week at a desk in
the Ministry ("I have my own telephone"), and on
Sundays he stayed home reading ("Among your
writers, the powerful one is A. J. Cronin. But Sholikov
is more powerful, yes?"). Home was an apartment on
the outskirts of Moscow where he lived with his family
and, as he was unmarried ("My stipend is not yet

equal to the aspiration''), shared a bedroom with his brother.

The conversation moved with an increasing ease; he ate a piece of Hershey, he laughed, his heels clicked; and then I offered him some books. They were stacked on the table, and his eyes continually strayed toward them, a gaudy collection of twenty-five-cent thrillers mixed in with Edmund Wilson's *To the Finland Station,* a history of the rise of Socialism, and Nancy Mitford's biography, *Madame de Pompadour.* I told him he could have them, if he liked.

At first, he was pleased. Then, as he reached for the books, his hands hesitated, withdrew, and his personal tic started; more shrugs, shrinkings, until he was swallowed again in the looseness of his clothes. ''I have not the time,'' he said regretfully. Afterwards, there seemed nothing left to say. He informed me that my passport was in order, and left.

Between midnight and two in the morning, The Blue Express stood still in a railroad siding near Moscow. The exterior coldness had stolen into the cars, forming lenses of ice on the inside surface of the window-panes; looking out, one saw merely spectral diffusions, as if your vision were deformed by cataracts. As soon as the train left Moscow, a restless mood rippled through the compartments; those who had been asleep wakened, began to flutter about like chickens tricked by a false dawn. The stay-ups poured another drink and breathed a second wind. Already, the pendulum was swinging toward the tensions of arrival.

Miss Thigpen woke up, calling, "Earl! Earl!" as though she'd had a bad dream.

"Gone," said Miss Ryan, who was curled in her berth nursing a brandy and reading Mickey Spillane. "He's out defying the law. Somebody's running a bootleg Tonk in the next car."

"That's no way to do. Earl ought to be getting his rest," said Miss Thigpen grouchily.

"Give him hell," Miss Ryan advised her. "He's *got* to marry you."

"Nancy, *quelle heure est-il?*"

"Twenty to four." At four Miss Thigpen again inquired the time; and again at ten past. "For God's sake, Helen. Either get a watch or take an *Oblivon.*"

Miss Thigpen kicked back her covers. "No sense trying. I'm better off dressed." It took her an hour and twenty-five minutes to select her costume and apply the right proportions of cosmetics and perfume. At five thirty-five she put on a feathered hat with a veil and sat down on her berth, completely clothed except for stockings and shoes. "I'm worried sick what to wear on my legs. I don't want to be poisoned," she said. Her fear was founded on a memo the Russians had issued to the ladies of the company on the subject of nylon hosiery. In conditions of severe cold, nylon, they announced, had a tendency to disintegrate, which might cause nylon poisoning. Miss Thigpen rubbed her naked legs and groaned. "What kind of place *is* this we're going? Where a lady's stockings fall to pieces on the street and maybe kill her?"

"Forget it," said Miss Ryan.

"But the Russians . . ."

"How the hell would they know? They don't have any nylons. That's why they say it."

It was eight in the morning before Jackson returned from his Tonk game. "Earl," said Miss Thigpen, "is this how you're going to do after we're married?"

"Sweet-girl," he said, wearily climbing into his berth, "the cat has howled his last. He's zero point zero. Ooble-ee-dood out."

Miss Thigpen was unsympathetic. "Earl, don't you dare go to sleep now. We're almost there. Go to sleep for such a little bit and you'll wake up an ugly mess."

Jackson muttered and drew a blanket over his head.

"Earl," said Miss Ryan softly, "I suppose you know they're going to make newsreels at the station?"

Very shortly afterwards, Jackson had shaved, changed shirts, and arrayed himself in a caramel-colored fur coat. He owned a hat of the same fur that he'd had "custom-made" fedora-style. While working his hands into a pair of gloves with holes along the fingers to reveal his rings, he gave his fiancée instructions on how to handle the expected cameras: "See, honey, we don't want to get stuck with a lot of still-men. That's a waste of time when they're busting out the flicker stuff." He scratched at the window with his jeweled fist, and squinted out; it was nine-five and still pitch-black, not the ideal color for photography. But half an hour later the darkness had turned to steel-grey mist and one could see the blueness of lightly falling snow.

One of the Ministry's representatives, Sascha, passed through the car, knocking at compartment doors. "Ladies and gentlemen, in twenty minutes we are arriving Leningrad."

I finished dressing and squeezed my way into the crowded corridor, where an excitement was moment by moment accelerating like the wheels of the train. Even Twerp, shawl-wrapped and hugged in Miss Putnam's arms, was prepared to disembark. Mrs. Gershwin was more prepared than Twerp. She bristled with mink, was frosted with diamonds, and her curls peeked charmingly from under a rich soft sable hat. "The hat, darling? I bought it in California. I've been saving it for a surprise. You do, love? How sweet of you, darling. *Darling* . . ." she said, an abrupt silence adding volume to her voice, "we're *there!*"

A stunned instant of disbelief, then a collective pushing toward the vestibule. The sad-eyed car attendant, stationed there to receive his tips, found himself not only ignored but also crushed against the wall. Alert as horses at the starting gate, Jackson and John McCurry jockeyed by the exit for position. McCurry is the heftier of the two, and when the door opened, he was the first man out.

He stepped straight into a grey throng, and a flash bulb's pop. "Bless you," said McCurry, as women vied to thrust bouquets into his hand. "Bless your little pointed heads."

"As we arrived, there were many birds flying about —black and white," wrote Warner Watson, as he later recorded the scene in his diary. "The white ones are *sakaros*. I write it down for my bird-watching friends. We were greeted by many friendly Russians. The women and men (of the company) were given bouquets of flowers. I wonder where they got them this time of year. Pathetic little bouquets like those made by a child."

Miss Ryan, also the keeper of a diary, wrote: "Official welcoming party of giant men and shabby ladies dressed more to meet a coffin than a theatrical company (black clothes, grey faces) but perhaps that's what they *were* doing. My useless plastic galoshes kept falling off, making it impossible to elbow efficiently through the press of microphones, cameras, and those battling to get at them. The Breens were on hand, Robert still half asleep but Wilva smile-smiling. At the head of the quay, dull brass letters spelled out LENINGRAD—and then I knew it was true."

The poet, Helen Wolfert, composed for her journal

a lengthy description. Here is an excerpt: "As we advanced along the platform to the exit, two columns of people stood on either side, applauding. When we reached the street a press of spectators closed in on us. Policemen pushed them away to let us pass but the people in return pushed them with equal vigor. The actors responded to the warmth and bustle and welcome with grace, graciousness, expansiveness and flare. If the Russian people fell in love with them, they weren't alone. I fell in love with them myself."

Perhaps a few footnotes should be added to these entries. The persons Miss Ryan refers to as "giant men and shabby ladies" were a hundred or more of Leningrad's leading theatrical artists who had been organized to meet the train. Remarkably, none of them had known in advance that *Porgy and Bess* had a Negro cast, and before the committee could rearrange their bewildered faces into expressions of positive welcome, the company were halfway out of the station. The "press of spectators" noted by Mrs. Wolfert consisted of ordinary citizens whose presence was the result of an item printed in the local edition of the previous day's *Izvestia*. "A touring American opera company will arrive by train tomorrow morning in Leningrad. It is expected they will perform here." These two lines were, by the way, the first publicity the Soviet press had given Breen's venture; but, despite its meager detail, the announcement had proved sufficiently intriguing to attract the at least one thousand Leningraders who lined the length of the station, cascaded down a flight of stairs and spilled into the street. I was less aware of the "warmth and bustle" that impressed Mrs. Wolfert. Except for light sprinklings of applause, the crowd, so it seemed to me, watched the exiting cast with immense silence, an almost catatonic demeanor that provided few clues as to what they thought of the American parade—Mrs. Gershwin, loaded with more bouquets than a bride; small Davy Bey, dancing an impromptu Suzy-Q; Jackson dispensing royal waves, and John McCurry walking with his hands clenched above his head like a prize fighter.

While the Russian reaction may have been inscrutable, the official Company Historian, Leonard Lyons, had a very definite opinion of his own. Taking professional note of the scene, he shook his head. "It hasn't been handled right. No showmanship. Why, if Breen knew his business," he said, passing through the door of the station, "we would've come out singing!"

Part II
The Muses
Are Heard

The Leningrad premiere of *Porgy and Bess,* an event expected to reap international publicity, was planned for the evening of Monday, December 26, which gave the company five days to prepare and rehearse, a sufficient time considering that the show had been touring the world nearly four years. But Robert Breen, the production's director, was determined that the audience at the Leningrad premiere would see the finest possible rendering of the Negro opera. Breen, and his energetic partner-wife, Wilva, and their chief assistant, the gentle, yet highly strung Warner Watson, were confident that the Russians would be "stunned" by the musical folk tale, that they would "never have seen anything like it." Several observers, though sympathetic, were not as sure. However looked at, by the Americans or by their Russian sponsors, the opening night promised to be one of the most suspenseful in theatrical annals. But that event was, on the morning of arrival, over a hundred hours away; and after the company had been driven in chartered buses from the Leningrad terminal to the Hotel Astoria, their feelings of suspense were centered around room accommodations.

The Astoria, situated on the impressive expanse of St. Isaac's Square, is an Intourist hotel, which means that it is run by the Soviet agency in control of all hotels where foreigners are permitted to stay. The Astoria justifiably claims to be the best hotel in Leningrad. Some think it the Ritz of all Russia. But it

contains few concessions to Western ideas of a deluxe
establishment. Of these, one is a room off the lobby that
advertises itself as an *Institut De Beauté,* where
guests may obtain *Pedicure, Manicure,* and *Coiffeur
pour Madame.* The *Institut,* with its mottled whiteness, its painful appurtenances, resembles a charity
clinic supervised by not too sanitary nurses, and the
coiffeur that Madame receives there is liable to leave
her hair with a texture excellent for scouring pans.
There is also on the lobby floor a trio of restaurants,
each leading into the other, cavernous affairs cheerful as airplane hangars. The center one is Leningrad's
smartest restaurant, and in the evenings, from eight
till midnight, an orchestra plays Russian jazz for a
local *haut monde* who seldom dance but sit morosely
counting the bubbles in syrupy glasses of Georgian
champagne. The hotel's Intourist office is located behind a low counter in the main lobby; its dozen desks
are so arranged that the employees have a broad
view, which simplifies their task of keeping tabs on
the comings and goings of the guests. It is a job they
have made still simpler, or foolproof, by stationing
dormitory matrons on each of the residential floors,
vigilantes who are on duty from dawn to dawn, never
allowing anyone to leave his room without giving him
the key, and constantly, like human punch-clocks, recording ins and outs in a bulky ledger. Perhaps
Houdini could've eluded them, but it is hard to see
how, since they sit at desks that face both the stair-

case and the elevator, an ancient bird cage that creaks on its cables. Actually, there is a rear, unguarded staircase connecting the upper floors with a remote side-lobby; and for the clandestine visitor, or the resident wishing to depart unnoticed, this would make the ideal route. Would, except that it is barricaded top to bottom with wooden fences reinforced by old settees and armoires. It might be that the management can find nowhere else to stash these pieces of furniture. Certainly there is no more room in the rooms. For the average Astoria abode is like the annex in a Victorian attic where some poor relation lives buried among the family discards: a miasma of romantic marble statuary, weak-bulbed lamps with tulle shades like ballerina skirts, tables, several of them, covered with Oriental carpeting, chairs galore, plush settees, armoires that could store steamer trunks, flower-papered walls kaleidoscopic with gilt-framed paintings of fruit and country idylls, beds concealed in cavelike alcoves behind dank velvet curtains: all this crammed into a tomb-dark, unventilated area (you can't open the windows in winter, and wouldn't want to if you could) quadruple the size of a train compartment. The hotel has grander quarters, of course, suites with five and six rooms, but the effect of the décor is the same, merely more abundantly so.

Nevertheless, the majority of the *Porgy and Bess* company were most approving of the Astoria, many because they had anticipated "something so much *worse"* and, instead, found their rooms "cozy," "kind of atmospheric" or, as the production's sophisticated publicist, Willem Van Loon, put it, "Full of art-nouveau charms. Really me!" But when the troupe first entered the lobby of the hotel, already milling with Chinese dignitaries and high-booted Cossacks, actual occupancy of these rooms was, in some instances, distant and debatable.

The Astoria's assigning of the rooms and, particularly, the suites seemed to be governed by a protocol, or lack of one, that embittered rather a few. Nancy Ryan volunteered a theory that the Russians had arrived at their system of room distribution by consulting Everyman Opera's payroll: "The less you get the more they give you." Whatever the reason, several of the leading players and prominent personalities, who were traveling as guests of the company, thought it "grotesque" and "crazy, man, crazy" that stagehands and wardrobe mistresses, carpenters and electricians were being led straight-away to the V.I.P. apartments, while they, the "real people," were supposed to content themselves with the hotel's backwater leftovers. "Are they kidding?" said Leonard Lyons. Another company guest, the New York financier, Herman Sartorius, had valid cause to complain; he'd been assigned no room at all. Nor had Mrs. Gershwin, who sat on her luggage in the lobby being soothed by Wilva Breen and Warner Watson.

"Don't you worry, baby," said Mrs. Breen, who

had arrived the night before by plane and was ensconced with her husband in six rooms of Astorian splendor. "The Russians may be slow, they may get things a little mixed up, but everything comes out straight in the end. Look what happened when I went to Moscow," she added, referring to a visit she had made to Moscow the previous October in connection with the present tour. "It took me nine days to do two hours' work. But everything came out fine in the end."

"Sure, Lee," said Warner Watson, brushing down his greying crew-cut with an agitated hand. "Sure, honey, we'll get this room business fenced in."

"Darling, I'm perfectly happy, darling," Mrs. Gershwin assured them. "I just think it's so wonderful *being* here."

"To think we really made it," said Mrs. Breen, beaming round her. "And what sweet, kind, adorable people. Wasn't that adorable when the train arrived?"

"Adorable," said Mrs. Gershwin, glancing at the mass of wilting bouquets that had been given her at the station.

"And the hotel's simply beautiful, isn't it?"

"Yes, Wilva," said Mrs. Gershwin blankly, as though her friend's enthusiasm was beginning to tire her.

"You'll have a beautiful room, Lee," said Mrs. Breen, and Warner Watson added, "If you don't like it, you can change it. Anything you want, Lee, we'll get it fenced in."

"Darling, please. It's not important, Not the tiniest bit. If they'll just put me *some*where, I wouldn't dream of moving," said Mrs. Gershwin, who was destined, in the course of the next few days, to insist on changing her accommodations three times.

The Ministry of Culture's delegation, headed by Nikolai Savchenko, the businesslike, formidable six-footer, were now in a whirl of pacifying, rectifying, promising everyone they would get the rooms they deserved. "Patience," pleaded one of them, the middle-aged Russian interpreter called Miss Lydia. "Do not contribute to the misery. We have plenty rooms. No one will stride the streets." Nancy Ryan said she wouldn't mind striding the streets, and suggested to me that we escape the confusion in the lobby by taking a walk.

St. Isaac's Square is hemmed on one side by a canal stemming from the Neva, a river that in winter threads through the city like a frozen Seine, and on the other by St. Isaac's Cathedral, which is now an antireligious museum. We walked toward the canal. The sky was sunless grey, and there was snow in the air, buoyant motes, playthings that seethed and floated like the toy flakes inside a crystal. It was noon, but there was no modern traffic on the square except for a car or two and a bus with its headlights burning. Now and then, though, horse-drawn sleds slithered across the snowy pavement. Along the embankments of the Neva, men on skis silently passed, and mothers aired their babies, drag-

ging them in small sleds. Everywhere, like darting
blackbirds, black-furred school children ice-skated on
the sidewalks. Two of these children stopped to inspect
us. They were twins, girls of nine or ten, and they wore
grey rabbit coats and blue velvet bonnets. They had
divided a pair of skates between them, but by holding
hands and pushing together, they managed very well
on one skate apiece. They looked at us with pretty
brown puzzled eyes, as though wondering what made
us different: Our clothes? Miss Ryan's lipstick? The
soft waves in her loose blond hair? Most foreigners in
Russia soon become accustomed to this: the slight
frown of the passer-by who is disturbed by something
about you that he can't at once put his finger on, and
who stops, stares, keeps glancing back, even quite often
feels compelled to follow you. The twins followed us
onto a footbridge that crossed the Neva, and watched
while we paused to look at the view.

The canal, no more than a snow ditch, was a sporting
ground for children whose laughing shrillness com-
bined with a ringing of bells, both sounds carrying on
the strong, shivery winds that blow from the Bay of
Finland. Skeleton trees, sheathed in ice, glittered
against the austere fronts of palaces that lined the
embankments and stretched to the distant Nevsky
Prospekt. Leningrad, presently a city of four million,
the Soviet Union's second largest and northernmost
metropolis, was built to the taste of the Czars, and
Czarist taste ran to French and Italian architecture,

which accounts not only for the style but also for the coloring of the palaces along the Neva and in other old quarters. Parisian blacks and greys predominate, but suddenly, here and there, the hot Italian palette intervenes: a palace of bitter green, of brilliant ochre, pale blue, orange. A few of the palaces have been converted into apartments, most are used for offices. Peter the Great, who is given high marks by the current regime because he introduced the sciences to Russia, would probably approve the myriad television aerials that have settled like a swarm of metal insects on the roofs of his once Imperial city.

We crossed the bridge and wandered through opened iron gates into the deserted courtyard of a blue palace. It was the beginning of a labyrinth, an arctic Casbah where one courtyard led into another via arcades and tunnels and across narrow streets snow-hushed and silent except for sleigh horses stamping their hooves, a drifting sound of bells, an occasional giggle from the twins, still trailing behind us.

The cold was like an anesthetic; gradually, I felt numb enough to undergo major surgery. But Miss Ryan refused to turn back. She said, "This is St. Petersburg, for God's sake. We're not just walking anywhere. I want to see as much as I can. And I'd better. From now on, you know where *I'll* be? Locked in a room typing a lot of nonsense for the Breens." But I saw that she couldn't last much longer, her face was drunkard-red, a frostbite spot whitened the tip of her nose. Minutes later, feeling its first sting, she was ready to seek the Astoria.

The trouble was, we were lost. It amused the twins greatly to see us rotating round the same streets and courtyards. They screeched and hugged each other with laughter when we came on an old man chopping wood and begged him for directions by swinging our arms like compass needles and shouting, *Astoria! Astoria!* The woodchopper didn't understand; he put down his axe and accompanied us to a street corner, where we were required to repeat our pantomine for three swarthy friends of his, none of whom got the point, but nevertheless beckoned us up another street. On the way, out of curiosity, we were joined by a gangly boy carrying a violin case, and a woman who must have been a butcher, for over her coat she was wearing an apron splattered with blood. The Russians babbled and argued; we decided they were taking us to a police station, and neither of us cared, as long as it was heated. By now, the moisture in my nose had frozen, my eyes were unfocused with cold. Still, I could see well enough to know that abruptly we were back at the Neva Canal footbridge. I wanted to grab Miss Ryan's hand and run. But she felt our entourage had been so faithful they deserved to see the mystery solved. From woodchopper to violinist, the procession, led by the twins who skated ahead like pied pipers, convoyed us across the square and straight to the Astoria's entrance. While they surrounded one of the Intourist limousines that stay parked in front of the hotel, and began to question its chauffeur about us, we rushed inside, collapsed on a bench and sucked the warm air like divers who have been too long underwater.

Leonard Lyons walked by. "Looks like you've been out," he said. Miss Ryan nodded, and Lyons, lowering his voice, asked, "Anybody follow you?"

"Yes," said Miss Ryan, *"crowds."*

A company bulletin board had been installed in the lobby. Attached to it were announcements concerning the company's rehearsal schedule, and a list of entertainments their Soviet hosts had planned for them, which included, in the days before the premiere, ballet and opera performances, a ride on the new Leningrad subway, a visit to the Hermitage Museum, and a Christmas party. Under the heading PROMPTLY, the dining hours had also been posted, and these, influenced by the fact that in the Russian theatre matinées start at noon and evening performances at eight, were listed as: Breakfast 9:30 A.M., Lunch 11:00 A.M., Dinner 5 P.M., Evening snack 11:30 P.M.

But at five on that first evening, I was enjoying a hot tub too much to bother about dinner. The bathroom, which belonged to the third-floor room assigned to me, had peeling sulphur walls, a cold radiator, and a broken toilet that rumbled like a mountain brook. The tub itself, circa 1900, was splotched with rust stains, and the water that poured from its taps was brown as iodine; but it was warm, it made a wonderful steam, and I basked in it, idly wondering if downstairs in the bleak dining room the company were at last being treated to caviar and vodka, shashlik, blinis and sour cream. (Ironically, as I learned later, they were receiving the same menu that had been served at every meal on the train: yogurt and raspberry soda, broth, breaded veal cutlets, carrots and peas.) My water-logged drowsing was interrupted when the telephone rang in the outer room. I let it go awhile, the way you might if you were sitting in a bath at home. Then I realized I wasn't home, remembered that, looking at the telephone earlier, I'd thought what a dead object it was to me in Russia, as useless as if the wires were cut. Naked and dripping, I picked up the receiver to hear the interpreter, Miss Lydia, telling me I had a call from Moscow. The telephone was on a desk next to the window. In the street below, a regiment of soldiers marched by singing a military song, and when Moscow came through I could hardly hear for the robust boom of their voices. The caller was someone I'd never met, Henry Shapiro, a United Press correspondent. He said, "What's going on there? Anything'd make a story?" He told me he'd been intending to travel to Leningrad for "the big story," the *Porgy and Bess* premiere, but now he couldn't, because he had to cover "another opening," the Supreme Soviet, which was happening in Moscow the same night. He would therefore appreciate it if he could call again on Monday after the premiere and have me report to him "how it went, what really happened." I said all right, I'd try. The call, and the shock of standing unclothed in a cold room, had brought me back to life. The company were expected to attend a ballet, and I started to get dressed for it. There was a problem here. The Breens had decreed that the men should wear black-tie, and the ladies short evening dresses. "It's more respectful," said Mrs. Breen, "and besides, Robert and I like everything to be gala." There was an opposing clique who felt that the Breens' pronouncement would, if obeyed, make them look "ridiculous" in a country where no one dressed formally for any occasion whatever. I compromised by putting on a grey flannel suit *and* a black tie. While dressing, I moved around the room straightening some of the fruit and flower paintings that clotted the walls. They were rather atilt, owing to an inspective visit from Leonard Lyons, who was convinced the Astoria's rooms were wired for sound. Lyons' theories were shared by most of the company, which was not remarkable, considering that two American diplomats from the Moscow Embassy had told them at a briefing in Berlin that, during their Russian visit, they should "assume" their rooms would be wired and their letters opened. Even Breen, who called the diplomatic advice "a lot of blah," had unwittingly encouraged the company's suspicions by declaring that, regardless of what anyone might individually feel, he hoped in correspondence they simply would write how "interesting" Russia was and what a "good time" they were having; this, some pointed out, was a contradiction, for why would Breen make such a request if he, too, didn't believe they were living in an atmosphere of microphones and steam kettles?

On my way out, I stopped at the floor desk and handed my key to the guardian, a plump pale woman with a kewpie-doll smile who wrote in her ledger *224–1900:* the number of my room and hour of departure.

Downstairs, there was a row in progress. The company, dressed and ready to leave for the ballet, stood around the lobby like mortified figures in a tableau, while one of the cast, John McCurry, a husky bull-like man, stomped about yelling, "Goddam if I will. I'm not gonna pay any goddam crooked somebody seven bucks fifty to baby sit anybody." McCurry was complaining of the price a Russian baby sitter was charging to stay with his four-year-old daughter while he and his wife went to the ballet. At a cost of thirty rubles per sitter, Intourist had supplied a batch to all the parents of the troupe's six children; they had even arranged one for Twerp, the boxer puppy belonging to the production's wardrobe mistress. Thirty rubles, at the exchange of four to one, amounts to $7.50, a stiff tariff; but actually to the Russian, thirty rubles has a buying power equivalent to $1.70, and the Russians, who had only this modest fee in mind, couldn't fathom why McCurry was causing such a scene. Savchenko, head man from the Ministry of Culture, was rosy with indignation, Miss Lydia white. Breen spoke sharply to McCurry, and McCurry's wife, a shy woman whose eyes are usually downcast, told him if he would please be quiet she would remain home with the child. Warner Watson and Miss Ryan hustled everyone out of the lobby and onto the two buses that had been chartered for the duration of their Leningrad stay.

Later, Breen apologized to Savchenko for the "conduct" of a few members of the company. The apology was intended to cover more than the McCurry incident. Free liquor was not included in the contract that had been drawn up between the Ministry of Culture and Everyman Opera, Inc. Savchenko was distressed because several persons had ordered drinks brought to their rooms and refused to pay for them, fought and insulted the waiters. Further, it had come to Savchenko's attention that many of the Americans were referring to him and his staff as "spies." Breen, too, felt that this was "unwarranted and outrageous," and Savchenko, in accepting his apologies, said, "Well, of course, in a company this size, we must expect some who will fall below the mark."

The ballet was at the Mariinsky theatre, which has been renamed, though no one calls it that, the Kirov, after the old revolutionary and friend of Stalin's whose assassination in 1934 is said to have initiated the first of the Moscow trials. Galina Ulanova, the

Bolshoi's prima ballerina, made her debut in this theatre, and the Leningrad Opera and Ballet Company, which is now installed there on a repertorial basis, is considered first-class by Soviet critics. Except for the Fenice in Venice, a theatre it somewhat resembles in its eighteenth-century size and style and heating system, I think it the most beautiful theatre I've seen. Unfortunately, the old seats have been replaced by wooden ones, rather like those in a school auditorium, and their harsh, natural color makes too raw a contrast against the subtle greys and silvers of the Mariinsky's simplified rococo interior.

Despite the chilliness of the theatre, everyone, ladies included, were required to leave their coats at the cloakroom; even Mrs. Gershwin was forced to part with her mink, for in Russia it is thought uncultured, *nye kulturni* at its extremest, to enter a theatre, restaurant, museum, any such place, wearing a coat or wrap. At the moment, the principal sufferer from the ruling was Miss Ryan. A tall, striking blonde, Miss Ryan was wearing a low strapless dress that hugged her curves cleverly; and as she swayed down the aisle, masculine eyes swerved in her direction like flowers turning toward the sun. For that matter, the entrance of the entire company was creating a mass stir in the crowded audience. People were standing up to get a better view of the Americans and their black ties, silks and sparkles. Much of the attention was centered on Earl Bruce Jackson and his fiancée, Helen Thigpen. They were sitting in the Royal Box, where a hammer-and-sickle blotted out the Imperial crest. Jackson, lolling his hand over the edge of the box so that his jewelry, a ring on every finger, could be seen to advantage, was slowly inclining his head right and left, like Queen Victoria.

"I'd be freezing, if I weren't so embarrassed," said Miss Ryan, as an usher seated her. "Just look, they think I'm *indecent*." One couldn't deny that there was a touch of criticism in the glances Miss Ryan's bare shoulders were receiving from surrounding Russian women. Mrs. Gershwin, who was wearing a becoming green cocktail dress, said, "I *told* Wilva Breen we shouldn't get all dressed up. I knew we'd look ridiculous. Well, darling, never again. But really, what *should* we wear?" she asked, looking about as if hunting fashion hints among the audience's melancholy, shapeless attire. "I didn't bring anything that wasn't pretty."

Sitting in the row ahead, there was one girl whose hair was neither plaited nor a sour bundle of string; she had an urchin-cut, which suited her curious, wild-faun face. She was wearing a black cardigan, and a pearl necklace. I pointed her out to Miss Ryan.

"But I *know* her," said Miss Ryan excitedly. "She's from Long Island, we went to Radcliffe together! *Priscilla* Johnson," she called, and the girl, squinting near-sighted eyes, turned around. "For God's sake, Priscilla. What are you doing here?"

"Gosh. Gee whiz. Nancy," said the girl, rubbing back her tomboy bangs. "What are *you* doing here?"

Miss Ryan told her, and the girl, who said that she too was staying at the Astoria, explained that she had been granted a lengthy visa to live in the Soviet Union and study Russian law, a subject that had interested her since Radcliffe, where she'd also learned the Russian language.

"But, darling," said Mrs. Gershwin, "how can anyone study Russian law? When it changes so often?"

"Gosh. Ha ha," said Miss Johnson. "Well, that's not the *only* thing I'm doing. I'm making a kind of Kinsey report. It's great fun, gosh."

"I should think," said Miss Ryan. "The research."

"Oh, that's easy," Miss Johnson assured her. "I just keep steering the conversation toward sex; and gee whiz, you'd be surprised what Russians think about it. Gosh, Nancy, the number of men who have mistresses! Or wished they did. I'm sending articles to *Vogue* and *Harper's Bazaar*. I thought they might be interested."

"Priscilla's a sort of genius," Miss Ryan whispered to me, as chandeliers dimmed and the orchestra conductor raised his baton. The ballet, in three acts with two intermissions, was called *Corsair*. The average Soviet ballet is far less concerned with dancing than with stupendous production, and *Corsair,* though a minor work in their repertory, involves as much change of scenery as the extravagant vaudevilles at Radio City Music Hall or the Folies Bergère, two theatres where *Corsair* would feel quite at home, except that the choreography and its execution are not up to the standards of the former, and the latter would never tolerate a scene of dancing slave girls swathed to the neck. The theme of *Corsair* is very similar to *The Fountains of Bahchisarai,* a poem of Pushkin's that the Bolshoi ballet has taken and swollen into one of its prize exhibits. In *Fountains,* an aristocratic girl is kidnaped by a barbaric Tartar chieftain and hauled off to his harem where, for three hours of playing time, many vile adventures befall her. In *Corsair,* this girl's twin sister undergoes somewhat the same ordeal; here she is the victim of a shipwreck (brilliantly simulated on stage with thunder, lightning, torrents of water crashing against the stricken vessel) who is captured by pirates, after which, for three hours, ditto. Both these tales, and countless like them, reflect a tendency in the contemporary Soviet theatre to rely on fantasy and legend; it would seem that the modern author who wishes to roam beyond the propagandist garden finds that the only safe path is the one that leads him into the forest of fairy stories. But even fantasy needs realistic underpinning, reminders of the recognizable, the human; without them, the power of life is not there, nor is art, a dual absence that occurs too often in the Soviet theatre, whose practitioners appear to believe that trick effects and technical wizardry can be made to supplant them. The Ministry of Culture frequently boasts that Russia is the sole country to have produced an artculture *en rapport* with its population. The reaction of the audience to *Corsair* was nothing to disprove the claim; every set, every solo brought chandelier-shaking rounds of applause.

The Americans were enthusiastic too. "Magnificent, a dream," Mrs. Breen told Mrs. Gershwin during an intermission spent in the Mariinsky's café-salon. The opinion was seconded by her husband. Yet while praising the ballet, Breen, a dapper man whose facial expressions alternate between boyish beamings and Buster Keaton calm, had a troubled flickering in his eyes, as though perhaps he was comparing the physical elaborateness of *Corsair* with *Porgy and Bess'* three simple changes of scenery; if lavish effects were the criterion, then Soviet audiences were certain to be disappointed with his production.

"Well, *I* don't like it," said Mrs. Gershwin rebelliously, as the Breens moved on to another group. "I can hardly keep awake. And I'm not going to say I like it if I don't. They (the Breens) would put the words in your mouth if they could." That, of course, was the difficulty of the Breens' position. Like parents who have taken their children on a visit to the neighbors, they lived in dreadful anticipation of *gaffes*, of breakage and misconduct.

Refreshments were on sale in the Mariinsky's café-salon: beer, liqueurs, raspberry soda, sandwiches, candy and ice cream. Earl Bruce Jackson said he was starving: "But, man, that ice cream costs a dollar a lick. And guess what they want for a little bitty piece of chocolate not big as your toe? Five-fifty." Ice cream, advertised by the Soviets to be a delicacy of their own contriving, started to become a national passion in the U.S.S.R. in 1939, when American machinery was imported for its making. Most of the customers jammed into the salon stood spooning it out of paper cups while watching the Americans pose for photographs, informal ones, balancing beer bottles on their foreheads, demonstrating the shimmy, doing imitations of Louis Armstrong.

At the second interval, I looked for Miss Ryan and found her backed into a corner, haughtily smoking a cigarette in a long holder and trying to pretend she was not the cynosure of puffy girls and leaden-faced women gathered to giggle and comment on her clinging gown and naked shoulders. Leonard Lyons, standing with her, said, "See, now you know how Marilyn Monroe feels. Would she be a wow here! She ought to get a visa. I'm going to tell her."

"Ohhhh," moaned Miss Ryan, "if *only* I could get my coat."

A man in his late thirties, clean-shaven, dignified, an athletic figure with a scholar's face, stepped up to Miss Ryan. "I should like to shake your hand," he said respectfully, "I want you to know how much my friends and I are looking forward to *Porgy and Bess.* It will be a powerful event for us, I can assure you. Some of us have obtained tickets for the first night. I," he said, smiling, "am among the fortunate." Miss

Ryan said she was pleased to hear that, and remarked on the excellence of his English, which he explained by saying that he'd spent several of the war years in Washington as part of a Russian Purchasing Commission. "But can you really understand me? It's been so long since I've had the opportunity of speaking—it makes my heart pound." One sensed, in the admiring intensity of his attitude toward Miss Ryan, that the pounding of his heart was not altogether due to the English language. His smile slackened as a fluttering light signaled the end of intermission; and urgently, as though spurred by an impulse he couldn't resist, he said, "Please let me see you again. I'd like to show you Leningrad." The invitation was directed to Miss Ryan, but by polite necessity included Lyons and myself. Miss Ryan told him to call us at the Astoria, and he jotted our names on a program, then wrote out his own and handed it to Miss Ryan.

"Stefan Orlov," Miss Ryan read, as we returned for the last act. "He's quite sweet."

"Yeah," said Lyons. "But he won't call. He'll think it over and get cold feet."

Arrangements had been made for the company to go backstage and meet the ballet artists. The final scene of *Corsair* is partly played on the deck of a ship hung with rope nets, and at the end of the performance, when the Americans came behind the curtain, there was such a congestion on stage that half the dancers had to stand on the ship's deck or climb the rope nets to get a glimpse of the Western colleagues whose entrance they cheered and applauded a full four minutes before enough quiet could be summoned for Breen to make a speech, which began, "It is *we* who should applaud *you*. Your thrilling artistry has produced an evening none of us will ever forget, and we only hope on Monday evening we can a little repay you for the pleasure you have given us." While Breen finished his speech, and the director of the Mariinsky made another, the little ballerinas, sweat seeping through their make-up, crept close to the American performers, and their painted eyes rolled, their lips ohd-ahd as they gazed at the visitors' shoes, shyly, then boldly, touched the dresses, rubbed bits of silk and taffeta between their fingers. One of them reached out and put her arm around a member of the company named Georgia Burke. "Why, precious-child," said Miss Burke, a warm, happy-natured woman, "hug me all you like. It's good to know somebody loves you."

It was nearer one than midnight when the company started the bus ride back to the Astoria. The buses, rolling refrigerators, had the same seating plan as those that operate on Madison Avenue. I sat on the long back seat between Miss Ryan and the interpreter, Miss Lydia. Street lamps, yellowing the snows of empty streets, flashed at the windows like wintry fire-flies, and Miss Ryan, looking out, said, "The palaces are so beautiful in the lamplight."

"Yes," said Miss Lydia, stifling a sleepy yawn, "the

private homes are beautiful." Then, as though suddenly awake, she added, "The *former* private homes."

The next morning I went shopping on the Nevsky Prospekt with Lyons and Mrs. Gershwin. Leningrad's principal street, the Nevsky is not a third the length of Fifth Avenue, but it is twice as wide; to get across its skidding aisles of traffic is a perilous chore and a rather pointless one, for the stores on either side of the street are all government-owned emporiums selling, in their different classifications, the same stock at the same prices. Bargain hunters, buyers on the lookout for "something a little different" would find shopping on the Nevsky a discouraging experience.

Lyons had set out with starry hopes of picking up "a nice piece of Fabergé" to take home to his wife. After the revolution, the Bolsheviks sold to French and English collectors almost all the jeweled eggs and boxes that Fabergé had created for the royal amusement; the few known examples of his work left in Russia are on display in Leningrad's Hermitage Museum and in the Armory at the Kremlin. Today, on the international market, the beginning price of a small Fabergé box is over two thousand dollars. None of this information impressed Lyons, who felt he was going to locate his Fabergé quickly and quite cheaply at a Commission Shop. Which was right thinking as far as it went, for if such an item existed, then a Commission Shop, a state-controlled pawn brokerage where a comrade can turn the last of his hidden heirlooms into spot cash, is probably the only place you would discover it. We visited several, drafty establishments with the going-gone sadness of auction halls. In one, the largest, a glass cabinet ran the length of the room, and the spectacle its contents presented, the conglomeration of spookily diverse objects, seemed a dadaist experiment. Rows of second-hand shoes, so worn the spectral shape of the previous owner's foot could be pathetically discerned, were neatly set forth under glass like treasures, which indeed they were at $50 to $175 a pair; a selection of headgear flanked the shoes, flapper cloches and velvet cartwheels; after the hats, the surrealistic variety and value of the cabinets' contents spiraled: a shattered fan ($30), a soiled powder-puff ($7), an amber comb with broken teeth ($45), tarnished mesh handbags ($100 and up), a silver umbrella handle ($340), an unexceptional ivory chess set with five pawns missing ($1,450), a celluloid elephant ($25), a pink plaster doll cracked and flaked as though it had been left in the rain ($25). All these articles, and yards more, were placed and numbered with a care that suggested an exhibition of mementos, the possessions of some dead beloved figure, and it was this, the reverence of the display, that made it poignant. Lyons said, "Who do you s'pose *buys* this stuff?" But he had only to look around him to see that there were those who, in lieu of anything else, found the moth-nibbled fan and the silver umbrella handle still fetching, still desirable, quite worth their quoted costs. According to the Russian calendar, Christmas was two weeks off, but Russians prefer to give gifts at New Year's, and the Commission Shops, like all the stores along the Nevsky, were packed with spenders. Though Lyons failed to flush any Fabergé, one pawnbroker came up with a unique nineteenth-century snuffbox, an immense topaz, hollowed and split in half. But the price, $80,000, was more than the customer had in mind.

Mrs. Gershwin, who intended giving a "really good" Christmas present to every member of the *Porgy and Bess* cast ("After all, darling, it's the company's fourth Christmas together, and I do want to show the darlings my appreciation"), still had a few odds and ends to finish off, though she'd carted a trunkload of gifts from Berlin. And so, struggling through the Nevsky crowds ("You can't deny there's a lot of vitality around here," said Lyons), we visited a furrier where the cheapest sable was a short jacket selling, or rather not selling, for $11,000. Then we stopped at an antique shop declared by Intourist to be Leningrad's most "elegant." The antiques turned out to be used television sets, an icebox, an old American electric fan, some battered pieces of Biedermeier, and a colossal number of oil paintings depicting scenes of historical event if not value. "What did you expect, darling?" said Mrs. Gershwin. "There's no such thing as Russian antiques. If there are, they're French." Inquiring for caviar, we went to two fancy-food stores, the local

Vendômes; there were pineapples from Africa, oranges from Israel, fresh lichee nuts from China; but no caviar. "Where, *where* did I get the idea it was the butter on the workingman's bread?" lamented Mrs. Gershwin, who said she'd settle for a cup of tea, a desire that shortly drove us into a Soviet version of Schrafft's. It was in a cellar, a dungeon where waitresses, wearing knee boots and tiaras made of doily paper, waded across slush-flooded floors carrying trays of ice cream and improbable pastry to gloomy groups of middle-aged women. But Mrs. Gershwin had to do without her tea, for there were no tables available, nor even space to stand.

So far, no one had made a single purchase. Mrs. Gershwin decided to try a department store. On the way, Lyons, who had a camera, paused often to take photographs, of match women and cherry-cheeked girls dragging Christmas trees, of street-corner flower stalls that in winter sell artificial roses, paper tulips stuck in flowerpots, as though they were real. Each of his photographic forays caused pedestrian traffic jams, a gallery of silent spectators who smiled, and sometimes scowled, when he took their pictures, too. Presently I noticed that there was one man who continuously showed up among the onlookers, yet did not seem part of them. He always stood at the rear, a chunky man with a crooked nose. He was bundled in a black coat and astrakhan cap and half his face was hidden behind the kind of windshield dark glasses skiers wear. I lost track of him before we reached the department store.

The store was reminiscent of a carnival alley, consisting, as it did, of counters and alcoves whose shelves seemed mostly stocked with shooting gallery prizes, the cheap familiar dolls, ugly urns, plaster animals, the toilette set bedded in a crumpling of white casket silk. Mrs. Gershwin, overcome by an odor of rancid glue, felt swift necessity to leave the "leather-goods" department, a swifter one to flee the perfume counter. A crowd began trailing us through the store, and when, in an alcove devoted to hats, I started trying on caps of ersatz Persian lamb, a good thirty grinning, jostling Russians ganged around demanding I buy this one, that one, themselves whisking models on and off my head and ordering the clerk to bring more, more, until hats were toppling off the counter. Someone bent to retrieve one from the floor; it was the man wearing ski glasses. The hat I bought, chosen at desperate random, proved later not to fit. A fake astrakhan, it cost $45; and, because of the complicated payment system that operates in all Soviet stores, from the humblest grocery to GUM's in Moscow, it required another forty minutes to complete the transaction. First, the clerk gives you a sales slip, which you carry to a cashier's booth, where you cool your heels while the cashier does her computations on an abacus, an efficient method no doubt, still some clever Soviet should invent the cash register; when the money has been paid, the cashier stamps the sales slip, and this you take back to the clerk, who by now is attending five other people; eventually, though, the clerk will accept the slip, go to check it with the cashier, come back, hand over your purchase, and direct you to a wrapping department, where you join another queue. At the end of this process, I was given my hat in a green box. "Please, darling," Mrs. Gershwin begged Lyons, who was tempted to buy a hat himself, *"don't* make us go through all that again."

Ski-glasses was nowhere in sight when we left the store. He turned up soon enough, however, at the edge of a group watching Lyons photograph peddlers selling Christmas trees in a snowy courtyard. It was there in the courtyard that I left the hatbox; I must have put it down to slap my numbed hands together. I didn't realize it was missing until many blocks later. Lyons and Mrs. Gershwin were game to go back and look for it. But that wasn't necessary. For as we turned around, we saw ski-glasses coming toward us, and dangling in his hand was the green hatbox. He gave it to me with a smile that twitched his crooked nose. Before I could think to say thank you, he'd tipped his cap and walked away.

"Well, ho ho—call that a coincidence?" crowed Lyons, a joyous shine livening his shrewd eyes. "Oh, I've had *him* spotted!"

"So have I," admitted Mrs. Gershwin. "But I think it's darling. Adorable. Simply adorable of them to take such good care of us. It makes you feel so protected. Well, darling," she said, as though determined Lyons should be persuaded to adopt her view, *"isn't* it a comfort to know you can't *lose* anything in Russia?"

At the Astoria, after lunch, I rode up in the elevator with Ira Wolfert, the former war correspondent who supposedly intended writing an article on Everyman Opera's tour for the *Reader's Digest*. "But I'm still looking for a story. What it seems to me is, is repetitious," Wolfert told me. "And you can't talk to anybody around here. Russians, I mean. It's giving me claustrophobia, every time I get into a political talk I keep getting the same old line. I was talking to Savchenko, he's supposed to be an intelligent guy, and I said to him, since this is a private talk, do you *honestly* believe all these things you're saying about America? You know, he was saying how Wall Street runs the country. But you can't talk to them. There's no realism in this social realism. Yesterday I was talking to a Russian—I won't define him, one of the guys we've met around here—and he slips me a note. This note asking me to call his sister in New York. He has a sister living there. Later on I see this guy on the street. I pull him down a side street and say, 'What the hell goes on here?' And he says, 'Everything's fine. Only it's better to be careful.' Everything's fine, but the guy's slipping me notes!" Wolfert bit hard on his pipe, and shook his head. "There's no realism. I'm getting claustrophobia."

Upstairs, I could hear the telephone ringing inside

my room as I unlocked the door. It was the man I'd met during an intermission at the ballet, Miss Ryan's admirer, Stefan Orlov. He said he'd been calling Miss Ryan but there was no answer. I suggested he try the Breens' suite, one room of which Miss Ryan was using as an office. "No," he said, sounding nervously apologetic. "I must not call again. So soon. But when may I see Nancy? *And* you?" he added, tactfully. I asked him if he would like to come by the hotel for a drink. There was a pause that lasted until I thought we'd been disconnected. Finally, he said, "That would not be convenient. But could you meet me, say, in an hour?" I said yes, where? He told me, "Walk around the cathedral. St. Isaac's. Keep walking. I will see you." He rang off without saying good-bye.

I went down to the Breens' suite to tell Miss Ryan of the invitation. She was delighted, "I knew he'd call," but crestfallen, "I'm stuck with six copies of a rush item," she said, inserting layers of paper and carbon into a portable typewriter. The rush item was a two-page letter written by Robert Breen and addressed to Charles E. Bohlen, the American Ambassador to Russia. It began by expressing gratitude over the fact that Ambassador and Mrs. Bohlen were coming to Leningrad for the *Porgy and Bess* premiere; but the bulk of the letter was in a tone of grieving complaint. Although the production's Soviet tour had the blessings of the U. S. State Department, it was not, contrary to the popular impression, under their official sponsorship. Indeed, the trip had been made financially possible by Russia's own Ministry of Culture. Nevertheless, Breen felt it was "a crying shame" no member of Ambassador Bohlen's staff had been permanently assigned to the company to observe "the day-to-day and minute-to-minute happenings, the individual contacts, and the spontaneous, warm incidents" that Breen considered necessary if the Embassy intended to "prepare properly the sort of full and valid report which rightfully should be expected on this unprecedented project." Breen wrote, "The need for such documentation concerns not only this good-will tour, important as it is, but also possible future cultural exchanges. No one can imagine the extreme lengths to which we have gone to provide smooth running—or the infinite amount of details which have to be foreseen and arranged if this type of exchange is to bear the fruit of its promise. The documentation should record not only our successes, but also those facets of public relations which might be improved, and the possible failures."

"Give my love to Stefan," Miss Ryan instructed, as I left to keep the appointment. "And if it turns out to be a spontaneous, warm incident be sure and tell me so I can put it in the *Porgy and Bess* log," she said, referring to an official journal of that title maintained by her employers.

It's a stone's throw from the Astoria to the semi-Gothic mass of St. Isaac's Cathedral. I left the hotel at exactly three-thirty, the time Orlov had said he would meet me. But on stepping out the door, I found myself confronting a pair of ski glasses. There was an Intourist Ziv parked at the curb, and the man was sitting in the front seat talking to a chauffeur. For a moment I thought of returning to the hotel; it seemed the sensible course if Orlov was concerned that his rendezvous be off the record. But I decided to stroll past the car and see what happened; as I went by, nerves and an unreliable sense of etiquette prompted me to nod at the man. He yawned and averted his face. I didn't look back until I'd crossed the square and was in the shadows of St. Isaac's. By then, the car was gone. I walked slowly around the cathedral, pretending to admire the architecture, though there was no reason to pretend anything, for the sidewalks were deserted. Still, I felt conspicuous, and not quite lawful. Night swept the sky like the black crows that wheeled and cawed overhead. On the third lap around, I began to suspect Orlov had changed his mind. I tried to forget the cold by counting my steps, and had ticked off two hundred and sixteen when, turning a corner, I came on a scene that made the flow of numbers stop like the hands of a dropped watch.

It was this: four men in black had a fifth man backed against the cathedral wall. They were pounding him with their fists, pushing him forward and hitting him with the full weight of their bodies, like football players practicing on a dummy. A woman, respectably dressed and carrying a pocketbook tucked under her arm, stood on the sidelines as though she were casually waiting while some men friends finished a business conversation. Except for the cawing of crows, it was like an episode from a silent film; no one made a sound, and as the four attackers relinquished the man, leaving him spread-eagled on the snow, they glanced at me indifferently, joined the woman and walked off without a word between them. I went over to the man. He was fat, too heavy for me to lift, and the drink on his breath would have killed scorpions. He was not bleeding and he was not unconscious, but he wanted to speak and couldn't; he gazed up at me like a deaf-mute attempting to communicate with his eyes.

A headlighted car pulled alongside the curb. The strip of black and white checks bordering its frame identified it as a taxi. The rear door opened, and Stefan Orlov called my name. Leaning in the door, I tried to explain what had happened and ask him to help the man, but he was impatient, he didn't want to listen, he kept saying, "Get in," and, "Will you *please* get in"; and at last, with a fury that shocked me, "You're an idiot!" he said, yanking me onto the seat. As the taxi swung in a U-turn, its headlights exposed the man sprawled on the sidewalk, his lifted hands plowing the air, like the claws of an insect cruelly tumbled on its back.

"I'm sorry," said Orlov, regaining a civil voice that also managed to sound sincerely remorseful. "But

other peoples's quarrels. They are not so much interesting, you understand. Now, enjoy yourself. We are
going to the Eastern.'' He commented on Miss Ryan's
absence and regretted ''deeply'' that she'd been unable to accept his invitation. ''The Eastern is where
you want to take a girl like Nancy. Very good food.
Music. A bit of Oriental atmosphere.'' After the clandestine nature of our meeting, it struck me as curious
that we were now proceeding anywhere as gay and
public as he described; and I said so. He was hurt. ''I
have no fears, but I'm not an idiot either. The Astoria
is a sensitive place. You understand? It's a nuisance
to go there. Why shouldn't I see you if I like?'' he said,
asking himself the question. ''You are a singer, I'm
interested in music.'' He was under the impression that
both Miss Ryan and myself were singers in the cast
of *Porgy and Bess*. When I corrected him, and told
him I was a writer, he seemed upset. He had lighted a
cigarette, and his lips, pursed to blow out the match,
tautened. ''Are you a correspondent?'' he asked, letting the flame burn. I said no, not what he meant by a
correspondent. He blew on the match. ''Because I hate
correspondents,'' he said, rather warningly, as
though I'd best not be lying to him. ''They're filthy.
And Americans, it's too bad to say, are the worst. The
filthiest.'' Now that he knew I was a writer, I thought
perhaps he saw the situation in a different, less harm-
less perspective, and so suggested that if the taxi
would take me within walking distance of the Astoria,

we could amicably part company then and there. He interpreted this as a protest to his opinion of American correspondents. "Please, you misunderstand. I admire so much the American *people*," he said, and told me that the years he'd spent in Washington "were of a happiness I never forget. The Russians who lived in New York were always very snobbish about the Russians who had to live in Washington; they said, 'Oh, my dear, Washington is so *boring* and provincial.'" He laughed at his grande-dame imitation. "But for me, I liked it there. The hot streets in the summer. Bourbon whiskey. I liked so much my flat. I open my windows and pour myself a bourbon," he said, as though reliving these actions. "I sit in my underwear and drink the bourbon and play the Vic loudly as I like. There is a girl I know. Two girls. One of them always comes by."

The so-called Eastern is a restaurant attached to the Hotel Europa, just off the Nevsky Prospekt. Unless a few desiccated potted-palms connote the Orient, I am at a loss to explain Orlov's contention that the place had a slant-eyed atmosphere. The atmosphere, if any, was a discouraging one of yellow-walled drabness and sparsely occupied tables. Orlov was self-conscious, he picked at his tie and smoothed his dark hair. While we crossed an empty dance floor, an ensemble, four musicians as spidery as the palms they stood among, were scratching out a waltz. We climbed a flight of stairs that led to a balcony where there were discreet dining booths. "I'm sure you think the Astoria is more elegant," he said, as we were seated. "But that is for foreigners and large snobs. Here is for smaller snobs. I am *very* small snob."

It worried me that he probably couldn't afford the Eastern at all. His overcoat featured a luxurious sable collar and he had a hat of gleaming sealskin. Still his suit was a poor, thin plaid and the laundered freshness of his white shirt somehow made more apparent its frayed cuffs and collar. But he gave sumptuous instructions to the waiter, who brought us a 400-gram carafe of vodka and a huge helping of caviar heaped in silver ice-cream dishes, toast and slices of lemon on the side. With a passing thought for Mrs. Gershwin, I dispatched every soft, unsalted, grey, pearly bead of it, and Orlov, marveling at the speed of my accomplishment, asked if I would like another serving. I said no, I couldn't possibly, but he saw that I could, and sent the waiter for more.

Meanwhile, he proposed toasts in honor of Miss Ryan. "To Nancy," he said, draining his glass, then, with a refill, "To Nancy. She is a beautiful girl"; and, again pouring, "That beautiful Nancy. Beautiful girl. Beautiful."

The succession of fast-gulped vodka flushed his pale, almost handsome face. He told me he could drink "a fool's fill" and not get drunk, but a gradual dimming of intelligence in his fine blue eyes belied the boast. He wanted to know if I thought Miss Ryan was partial to

him. "Because," he said, leaning forward in an attitude of excessive confidence, "she is a beautiful girl,
and I like her." I said yes, I gathered he considered
her highly. "But you think I'm an idiot? Because I'm
nearly forty and I'm married five years?" He spread
his hand on the table to show me a plain gold wedding
ring. "I would never do harm to my marriage," he
said piously. "We have two babies, little girls." He
described his wife as "not beautiful, but my principal
friend," and told me that, aside from the children, the
mutual interests they shared made the marriage "a
serious composition." Among professional classes in
Russia, it can be observed that persons seldom make
alliances with anyone outside their own field of work.
Doctors marry doctors; lawyers, lawyers. The Orlovs,
it seemed, were both mathematicians who taught at the
same Leningrad school. Music and the theatre formed
their main pleasures; they had taken turns, he said,
waiting in line to buy tickets for the *Porgy and Bess*
first-night, but in the end they had been allowed just
one ticket. "Now my wife pretends she doesn't want to
go. That is so I can go." The previous year they had
bought a television set as a New Year's present to each
other, but now they regretted having spent the money
on something "so boring and childish." He expressed
himself with equal harshness on the subject of Soviet
films. His wife, however, was fond of going to the *kino*,
but he himself would only be enthusiastic if ever again
they showed American pictures. ("I should like to

know. What has happened to that beautiful girl, Joan Bennett? And the other one, Ingrid Bergman? And George Raft? What a wonderful actor! Is he still alive?") Apart from this disagreement on the merits of movie going, his wife's tastes coincided with his at every point; they even, he said, enjoyed the same sport, "boating," and for several years had been saving to buy a small sailboat, which they intended docking at a fishing village near Leningrad where each summer they spent two months' vacation. "That is what I live for—guiding a boat through the poetry of our white nights. You must come back when the white nights are here. They are a true reward for nine months' dark."

The vodka was exhausted, and Orlov, after calling for a replenishment, grumbled that I wasn't keeping pace with him. He said it "disgusted" him to watch me "just tasting," and demanded that I "drink like a decent fellow or leave the table." I was surprised how easy it was to empty a glass in one swallow, how pleasant, and it appeared not to affect me except for a tickling warmth and a feeling that my critical faculties were receding. I began to think that after all Orlov was right, the restaurant did have an Oriental atmosphere, a Moorish coziness, and the music of the orchestra, scraping like cicadas among the palms, seemed to acquire a beguiling, nostalgic lilt.

Orlov, at the stage of repeating himself, said, "I'm a good man and I have a good wife," three times before he could reach the next sentence, which was, "But

I have strong muscles." He flexed his arms. "I'm passionate. A lusty dancer. On hot nights, with the window open, and the Vic playing loud as we like . . . and the Vic playing loud as we like. One of them always comes by. And we dance like that. With the window open on hot nights. That's all I want. To dance with Nancy. Beautiful. A beautiful girl. You understand? Just to dance. Just to . . . Where is she?" His hand swept the table. Silverware clattered on the floor. "Why isn't Nancy here? Why won't she sing for us?" With his head tilted back he sang, "Missouri woman on the Mississippi with her apron strings Missouri woman drags her diamond rings by her apron strings down the bad Missouri on the Mississippi blues . . ." His voice grew louder, he lapsed into Russian, a hollering still obscurely associated with the tune of "St. Louis Blues." I looked at my watch. To my astonishment it was nine o'clock. We'd been sitting in the Eastern almost five hours, which meant I couldn't be as sober as I reckoned. The realization and the proof of it struck simultaneously, like a pair of assassins who had been lying in wait. The tables seemed to slide, the lights swing, as though the restaurant were a ship riding a rough sea. At my request, insistence, Orlov asked for the check, but he went on singing while he counted out his rubles, sang his way down the stairs and waltzed by himself across the dance floor, ignoring the orchestra for his own accompaniment, "Missouri woman you're a bad Missouri woman on the Mississippi blues . . ."

In front of the Eastern there was a vendor selling rubber animals. Orlov bought a rabbit and handed it to me. "Tell Nancy from Stefan." Then he pulled me along a street that led away from the Nevsky Prospekt. As mud lanes replaced pavement it became clear that our destination was not the Astoria. For this was no neighborhood of palaces. Instead it was as though I were walking again through the slums of New Orleans, a district of dirt streets and broken fences, sagging wooden houses. We passed an abandoned church where wind wailed round the domes like a widow at the grave. Not far from the church, sidewalks resumed, and, with them, the city's imperial façade. Orlov headed toward the lighted windows of a café. The cold walk had quietened, somewhat sobered him. At the door, he said, "Here it is better. A workingman's place."

It was as if one had fallen into a bear pit. The body heat and beery breath and damp-fur smell of a hundred growling, quarreling, pawing customers filled the bright-lighted café. Ten and twelve men huddled around each of the room's half-dozen tables.

The only women present were three look-alike waitresses, brawny girls, wide as they were tall, and with faces round and flat as plates. In addition to waiting, they did duty as bouncers. Calmly, expertly, with an odd absence of rancor and less effort than it takes to yawn, they could throw a punch that knocked the stuffings out of men double their size. Lord help the man who fought back. Then all three girls would converge on him, beat him to his knees, literally wipe the floor with him as they dragged his carcass to the door and pitched it into the night. Some men, would-be customers decidedly persona non grata, never got into the café, for as soon as any of these undesirables appeared at the door the ladies of the establishment formed a flying, flailing wedge to drive him out again. Yet they could be courteous. At least they smiled at Orlov, impressed, I think, by his sable collar and expensive hat. One of them showed us to a table where she told two men, young jut-jawed bruisers wearing leather coats, to get up and give us their chairs. One was willing, the other argued. She settled his objections by snatching his hair and twisting his ear.

For the most part, only upper-strata restaurants are licensed to sell vodka, and since the café was not in that category, Orlov ordered Russian cognac, a brackish liquid that came in large tea glasses overflowing their brim. With the blitheness of a man blowing foam off a beer, he emptied a third of his glass and asked if the café "pleased" me, or did I think it "rough." I answered yes, and yes. "Rough, but not hooligan," he differentiated. "On the waterfront, yes, that is hooligan. But here is just ordinary. A workingman's place. No snobs." We had eight companions at the table and they took an interest in me, picked at me like magpies, plucked a cigarette lighter out of my hand, a scarf from around my neck, objects they passed from one to the next, glaring at them, grinning over them, and showing, even the youngest, rows of rotted teeth, wrinkles for which age could not account. The man nearest was jealous and wanted all my attention. It was impossible to guess how old he was, anywhere from forty to seventy. He had an eye missing and this circumstance enabled him to do a trick, which he kept forcing me to watch. It was meant to be a parody of Christ on the Cross. Taking a swallow of beer he would stretch his arms and droop his head. In a moment a trickle of beer came crying out the gaping redness of his hollow eye socket. His friends at the table thought it was an uproarious stunt.

Another favorite of the café was a boy who roamed around with a guitar. If you bought him a drink he'd sing you a song. He played one for Orlov, who translated it to me, saying it was the kind of song "we" like. It was the lament of a sailor longing for the village of his youth and a lost love called Nina. "The green of the sea is the green of her eyes." The boy sang well, with plaintive flamenco waverings in his voice. I sensed, though, that he was not concentrating on the lyrics. His thoughts and his gaze too were directed toward me. His white face had a sadness that seemed to be painted on, like a clown's. But it was his eyes that bothered me. Then I knew why. It was because they reminded me of the expression, the deaf-mute pleadings, in the eyes of the man left lying on the cathedral sidewalk. When he stopped playing, Orlov told him to sing another song. Instead the boy tried to speak to me.

"I . . . you . . . mother . . . man." He knew about ten words of English and he struggled to pronounce them. I asked Orlov to interpret, and as they talked together in Russian it was as though the boy were singing again. While his voice wove some sorrowful prose melody, his fingers tinkered with the strings of the guitar. Tears sprang to his eyes, and he rubbed them away with the flat of his palm, leaving grimy smudges like a child. I asked Orlov what he was saying. "It's not so much interesting. I'm not interested in politics." It seemed inconceivable the boy was talking politics, and when I persisted, Orlov was annoyed. "It's nothing. A nuisance. He wants you to help him."

Help was a word the boy understood. "Help," he said, nodding vigorously. "Help."

"Isn't he a nuisance?" said Orlov. "He says his father was English and his mother Polish, and because of this he says he's very badly treated in our country. He wants you to write the British Ambassador. Something like that. He wants to go to England."

"English man," said the boy, pointing at himself proudly. "Help." I didn't see how I could, and as he looked at me despair began to shade the hopeful shine of his wet eyes. "Help," he repeated reproachfully. "Help. Help."

Orlov gave him a coin and told him the name of a

song he wanted to hear. It was a comedy song with unending choruses, and though the boy drudged through it listlessly, even the waitresses laughed and roared out the key lines, which everybody seemed to know. The one-eyed man, angry that there should be such laughter for anything except his trick, climbed on his chair and stood like a scarecrow Jesus, beer oozing from the empty socket and dribbling down his cheek. At five minutes to midnight, closing time, the waitresses began to switch the lights on and off, warningly. But the customers kept the song going, clung to these last minutes, as though they loathed to trade the café's camaraderie for cold streets, the fierce lonely journeys homeward. Orlov said he'd walk me to St. Isaac's Square. But first, a final toast. He proposed, "To a long life and a merry one. Is that what they say?" Yes, I told him, that's what they say.

The boy with the guitar blocked our path to the door. Exiting customers were still warbling his song; you could hear their voices echoing down the street. And in the café the waitresses were shooing out the last die-hards, darkening the lights in earnest. "Help," said the boy, gently catching hold of my sleeve. "Help," he said, his eyes full on me, as a waitress, at Orlov's request, pushed him aside to let us by. "Help, help," he called after me, a door between us now, and the words a muted sound fading into nothing like the night-falling snow.

"I think he's a crazy person," said Orlov.

"New York could've been bombed, for all we know," said Leonard Lyons to the financier, Herman Sartorius, who was sitting next to him in a bus that was taking the company on a morning visit to the Hermitage Museum. "I've never been in a place I couldn't read a newspaper, find out what's going on in the world. A prisoner, that's how I feel." Sartorius, a tall, greying, solemnly courteous man, confessed that he too missed Western newspapers and wondered aloud if it would seem "not quite the correct thing" if he inquired at a Leningrad bank for the current New York Stock Exchange quotations.

As it happened there was a passenger seated behind them who could have supplied any information they wanted. It was his business to know what went on beyond the iron curtain, especially in America. A Russian, his name was Josef ("Call me Joe") Adamov, and he was in Leningrad to tape-record interviews with the *Porgy and Bess* cast for Radio Moscow, the station that beams broadcasts to countries outside the Soviet orbit. Adamov's talents are devoted to programs intended for American, or English-speaking, consumption. The programs consist of news reports, music, and soap operas sudsy with propaganda. Listening to one of these plays is a startling experience, not for the content, which is crude, but for the acting, which isn't. The voices pretending to be "average" Americans seem precisely that: one has absolute belief in the man who says he's a Midwest farmer, a Texas cowhand, a Detroit factory worker. Even the voices of "children" sound familiar as the crunch of Wheaties, the crack of a baseball. Adamov bragged that none of these actors had ever left Russia, their accents were manufactured right in Moscow. Himself a frequent actor in the plays, Adamov has so perfected a certain American accent that he fooled a native of the region, Lyons, who said, "Gee, I'm dumfounded, I keep wondering what's he doing so far from Lindy's." Adamov indeed seems to belong on the corner of Broadway and Fifty-first, a copy of *Variety* jammed under his arm. Although his slang needs dusting off, it is delivered with a bizarrely fluent side-of-the-mouth technique. "Me, I'm no museum-type guy," he said, as we neared the Hermitage. "But if you go in for all that creepy stuff, they tell me this joint's okay, really loaded." Swart, moon-faced, a man in his middle thirties with a jumpy, giggling, coffee-nerves animation, his shifty eyes grow shiftier when, under duress, he admits that his English was learned in New York, where he lived from the ages of eight to twelve with an émigré grandfather. He prefers to skate over this American episode. "I was just a kid," he says, as though he were saying, "I didn't know any better." A foreign resident in Moscow, who knows Adamov well, described him to me as "no fool. An opportunist with two fingers in every pie." And an Italian correspondent, another old Moscow hand, said, "Ah, si. Signor Adamov. The smiler with the knife." In short, Adamov is a successful man, which means, as it does elsewhere, though far more so in Russia, that he enjoys privileges unknown to the ordinary citizen. The one he values most is a two-room bachelor apartment in Moscow's Gorky Street, where he lives, to hear him tell it, the life of a Turk in his seraglio. "Gimme a buzz you come to Moscow, you wanta meet some cute kids." Meanwhile, he thought some members of the *Porgy and Bess* company were "pretty cute kids," particularly the saucer-eyed singer in the chorus named Dolores ("Delirious") Swann. At the museum, when the sight-seers were separated into battalions of twelve, Adamov made a point of joining Miss Swann in a group that included, among others, the Wolferts, Mrs. Gershwin, Nancy Ryan, Warner Watson and myself.

The Hermitage is part of the Winter Palace, which in recent years has been repainted the Imperial color, a frosty chartreuse-*vert*. Its miles of silvery windows overlook a park and a wide expanse of the Neva River. "The Winter Palace was started working 1764 and took seventy-eight years to finish," said the guide, a mannish girl with a brisk, whip-'em-through attitude. "It consists of four buildings and contains, as you see, the world's greatest museum. This where we are standing is the Ambassadorial Staircase, used by the ambassadors mounting to see the Czar."

In the ectoplasmic wake of those ambassadors our party followed her up marble stairs that curved under a filigree ceiling of white and gold. We passed through a splendid hall of green malachite, like a corridor under the sea, and here there were French windows where a few of us paused to look across the Neva at a misty-hazy view of that celebrated torture chamber, the Peter-Paul fortress. "Come, come," the guide urged. "There is much to see and we will not accomplish our mission if we linger at useless spectacles."

A visit to the treasure vault was the mission's immediate objective. "That's where they keep the ice, the *real* stuff: crown jools, all that crap," Adamov informed Miss Swann. A dragoon of stunted Amazons, several of them in uniform and wearing pistols strapped round their waists, guard the vault's bolted doors. Adamov, jerking a thumb toward the guards, told Warner Watson, "I'll bet you don't have any female cops in America, huh?"

"Sure," said Watson timidly. "We have policewomen, sure."

"But," said Adamov, his moist moon-face going scarlet with laughter, "not as fat as these, huh?"

While the vault's complicated steel doors were being unlocked, the guide announced, "Ladies will please leave their pocketbooks with the custodians." Then, as though to circumvent the obvious implication, "It is a matter of ladies causing damage dropping their pocketbooks. We have had that experience."

The vault is divided into three small, chandelier-lighted rooms, the first two entirely occupied by the museum's most unique display, a sophisticated panorama of Scythian gold, buttons and bracelets, cruel weapons, papery leaves and wreath garlands. "First-century stuff," said Adamov. "B.C. A.D. all that crap." The third room is intellectually duller, and much more dazzling. A dozen glass-enclosed cabinets (bearing the metal marker of their maker, Holland and Sons, 23 Mount Street, Grosvenor Square, London) afire with aristocratic souvenirs. Onyx and ivory walking sticks, musical birds that sing with emerald tongues, a lily bouquet made of pearls, another of ruby roses, rings and boxes that give off a trembling glare like heat waves.

Miss Swann sang, "But dee-*imonds* are a girl's best friend," and someone who shouted, "Where's that Earl Jackson?" was told, "Oh Earl, you know that cat wouldn't be up this hour of the day. But he's sure going to be sorry he missed this. Him feeling the way he does about sparkles."

Adamov planted himself in front of the cabinet containing one of the collection's few examples of Fabergé, a miniature version of the Czar's symbols of power: crown, scepter and orb. "It's gorgeous," sighed Miss Swann. "Don't you think it's gorgeous, Mr. Adamov?" Adamov smiled indulgently. "If *you* say so, kid. Personally, I think it's junk. What good does it do anybody?"

Ira Wolfert, chewing on an unlit pipe, was rather of Adamov's opinion. At least, "I hate jewelry," he said, glowering at a tray of blazing froufrou. "I don't know the difference between a zircon and a diamond. Except I like zircons better. They're shinier." He put an arm around his wife, Helen. "I'm glad I married a woman who doesn't like jewelry."

"Oh, I like *jewelry*, Ira," said Mrs. Wolfert, a comfortable-looking woman prone to expressing decisive notions in a tentative tone. "I like *creations*. But *this*, this is all trickery and show-off. It makes me ill."

"It makes me ill, too," said Miss Ryan. "But in quite a different way. I'd give anything for that ring —the tiger's eye."

"It makes me ill," Mrs. Wolfert repeated. "I don't call these things creations. This," she said, indicating a brooch of her own, a straightforward design in Mexican silver, "is what *I* call a creation."

Mrs. Gershwin was also making comparisons. "I wish I'd *never* come here," she said, forlornly fingering her diamonds. "I feel so dissatisfied, I'd like to go home and crack my husband on the head." Miss Ryan asked her, "If you could have any of this you wanted, what would you take?"

"All of it, darling," replied Mrs. Gershwin.

Miss Ryan agreed. "And when I got it home, I'd spread it on the floor and rip off my clothes and just *roll*."

Wolfert desired nothing, he simply wanted to "get the hell out of here and see something interesting," a wish he conveyed to the guide, who acquiesced by herding everyone to the door and counting them as they left.

Some six kilometers later, the group, its ranks thinned by fatigue cases, stumbled into the last exhibit hall, weak-legged after two hours of inspecting Egyptian mummies and Italian Madonnas, craning their necks at excellent old masters excruciatingly hung, poking about the sarcophagus of Alexander Nevsky, and marveling over a pair of Peter the Great's Goliath-large boots. "Made," said the guide, "by this progressive man with his *own* hands." Now, in the last hall, the guide commanded us to "go to the window and view the hanging garden."

"But where," bleated Miss Swann, "where *is* the garden?"

"Under the snow," said the guide. "And over here," she said, directing attention to the final item on the agenda, "is our famous The Peacock."

The Peacock, an exotic mechanical folly constructed by the eighteenth-century clockmaker, James Cox, was brought to Russia as a gift for Catherine II. It is housed in a glass cage the size of a garden gazebo. The focus of the piece is a peacock perched among the gilded leaves of a bronze tree. Balanced on other branches are an owl, a cock rooster, a squirrel nibbling a nut. At the base of the tree there is a scattering of mushrooms, one of which forms the face of a clock. "When the hour strikes, we have here a forceful happening," said the guide. "The peacock spreads her tail, and the rooster cackles. The owl blinks her eyes, and the squirrel has a good munch."

Adamov grunted. "I don't care what it does. It's dopey." Miss Ryan took him to task. She wanted to know why he should feel that way about an object of such "imaginative craftsmanship." He shrugged. "What's imaginative about it? A lot of jerks going blind so milady can watch a peacock fan her tail. Look at those leaves. Think of the work went into that. All for nothing. A nonutilitarian nothing. What'cha up to, kid?" he said, for Miss Ryan had started scribbling in a notebook. "What'cha doing? Putting down all the dumb things I say?" Actually, as Miss Ryan was surprised into explaining, she was writing a description of the clock. "Uh huh," he said, his voice not as genial as his smile, "you think I'm pretty dumb, don't you? Well, put this down. I'll tell you a good reason I don't like it. Because that peacock's gonna go on fanning her tail when I'm dust. A man works all his life, he ends up dust. That's what museums are, reminders of death. Death," he repeated, with a nervous titter that expanded into mirthless guffaws.

A gang of soldiers, part of another tour, approached The Peacock just as the hour chimed, and the soldiers, country boys with their heads shaved bald, their drab uniforms sagging in the seat like diapers, had the double enchantment of gaping at foreigners and watching the golden-eyed winkings of an owl, a peacock flash its bronze feathers in the wan light of the Winter Palace. The Americans and the soldiers crowded close to hear

the rooster crow. Man and art, for a moment alive together, immune to old mortality.

It was Christmas Eve. The translators from the
Ministry of Culture, under the supervision of their
chief, Savchenko, had personally set up a skinny fir
tree in the center of an Astoria dining room and dec-
orated it with hand-colored paper cards, wisps of tin-
sel. The members of the company, sentimental over
their fourth Christmas together, had gone on spending
sprees: a razzledazzle of cellophane and ribbon spread
in a knee-deep, twenty-foot circle round the tree. The
presents were to be opened at midnight. Long past
that hour, Miss Ryan was still in her room wrapping
packages and rummaging through suitcases selecting
from her possessions trinkets to take the place of gifts
she'd neglected to buy. "Maybe I could give the bunny
to one of the kids," she said, meaning the rubber rabbit sent her by Stefan Orlov. The rabbit nestled among
her bed pillows. She'd inked whiskers on its face and
on its side printed, STEFAN—THE BUNNY. "I guess not,"
she decided. "If I gave him away no one would ever
believe I'd snagged a Russian beau. *Almost* did."
Orlov had not telephoned again.

I helped Miss Ryan carry her presents down to the
dining room, where she was just in time for the end of
the gift-distributing. The children had been allowed to
stay up for the party, and now, hugging new dolls and

squirting water pistols filled with raspberry soda, they cycloned through the gaudy wrapping-paper debris. The grownups danced to the music of the Russian jazz band, which could be heard playing in the connecting main restaurant. Mrs. Breen whirled by, a bit of holiday ribbon floating round her neck. "Isn't it bliss?" she said. "Aren't you happy? After all, we don't spend *every* Christmas in Leningrad!" The waitresses, young English-language students who had volunteered to tend table for the American troupe, demurely refused invitations to dance. "Oh, come on, honey," one waitress was urged, "let's you and me melt that curtain together." Vodka, abetting the spirit of the occasion, had already melted the reserve of the Ministry of Culture representatives. They each had received presents from the company, and Miss Lydia, who had been given a compact, wanted to kiss everyone in sight. "It is too kind, so kind," she said, tirelessly examining her pudgy face in the compact's mirror.

Even the aloof Savchenko, a dour, glacial Santa Claus, or Father Frost, as the fellow is known in Russia, seemed after a while willing to forget his dignity, at any rate was unprotesting when a girl in the cast plumped herself on his lap, threw her arms around him and, between kisses, told him, "How come you want to look like a grumpy old bear when you're just a doll? A living doll, that's what you are, Mr. Savchenko." Breen, too, had affectionate words for the

Ministry of Culture executive. "Let's all drink to the man we can thank for this wonderful party," he said, hoisting a tumbler of vodka, "one of the best friends we have in the world, Nikolai Savchenko." Savchenko, wiping away lipstick, responded by proposing another toast. "To the free exchange of culture between the artists of our countries. When the cannons are heard, the muses are silent," he continued, quoting his favorite maxim. "When the cannons are silent, the muses are heard."

The radio man from Moscow, "Joe" Adamov, was busily tape-recording aspects of the party on a portable machine. Eight-year-old Davy Bey, solicited for a comment, said into Adamov's microphone, "Hello, everybody, happy Christmas. Daddy wants me to go to bed, but we're all having a grand time, so I'm not going. Well, I got a gun and a boat, only what I wanted was an airplane and not so many clothes. Any kids would like it, why don't they come over and play with us. We got bubble gum, and I know some good places to hide." Adamov also recorded "Silent Night, Holy Night," which the cast, gathered round the tree, sang with a volume that drowned the next-room thumping of the dance band. Ira Wolfert and his wife added their voices to the choir. The Wolferts, parents of adult children, had booked a telephone call to America. "All our children will be together tonight; tomorrow they go different ways," said Mrs. Wolfert when the caroling ended. "Oh, Ira," she squeezed her husband's hand, "that's the only present I want. For our call to come through." It never did. They waited till two, then went to bed.

After two, the Christmas party infiltrated the adjoining room, the Astoria's "night club," which is permitted to operate later than twelve on Saturdays, the only night of the week when patrons outnumber personnel. The Soviet habit of seating strangers together does not encourage uninhibited conversation, and the cavernous restaurant, occupied to near capacity by Leningrad's elite, was unreasonably subdued, the merest few, mostly young army and naval officers with their sweethearts, taking advantage of the orchestra's respectable rhythms. The rest, artists and theatrical personalities, groups of military Chinese, jowly commissars accompanied by their uncorseted, gold-toothed wives, sat around bored and uncaring as castaways on a Pacific atoll.

Earl Bruce Jackson took one look, and said, "Whatcha say, cats, let's get the snakes crawlin', put some hotcha in the pot, skin the beast and sprinkle pepper in his eyes." Whereupon five members of the company commandeered the bandstand. The hotel musicians had not the least objection to being ousted. They all were fans of American jazz, and one of them, a devotee of Dizzy Gillespie, had accumulated a large record collection by listening to foreign broadcasts and recording the music on discs made from old x-ray plates. Junior Mignatt spit into a trumpet, banana-fingered Lorenzo Fuller struck piano chords. Moses Lamar, a powerhouse with sandpaper lungs, stomped his foot, opened his mouth wide as an alligator. "Grab yo' hat 'n grab yo' coat, leave yo' worry on de do' step . . ." It was as though the castaways had sighted rescue on the horizon. Smiles broke out like an unfurling of flags, tables emptied onto the dance floor. ". . . just direct yo' feet . . ." A Chinese cadet tapped his foot, Russians packed close to the bandstand, riveted by Lamar's scratchy voice, the drumbeat riding behind it. ". . . to de sunny *sunny* SUNNY . . ." Couples rocked, swayed in each other's arms. ". . . side ah de streeeet!"

"Look at them zombies go!" said Jackson, and shouted to Lamar, "They're skinned, man, skinned. Throw on the gasoline and burn 'em alive. Ooble-ee-do."

Mrs. Breen, a smiling shepherd gazing at her flock, turned to Leonard Lyons. "You see. We've broken through. Robert's done what the diplomats couldn't." A skeptical Lyons replied, "All I say is, fiddles play while Rome burns."

At one of the tables I noticed Priscilla Johnson, the college friend of Miss Ryan's who was studying Russian law, and writing, so she said, articles on Soviet love life. She was sitting with three Russians, one of whom, a gnarled unshaven gnome with frothy black hair, splashed champagne into a glass and thrust it at me. "He wants you to sit down, and, gosh, you'd better," Miss Johnson advised. "He's a wild man, sort of. But fascinating." He was a Georgian sculptor, responsible for the heroic statuary in the new Leningrad subway, and his "wild man" quality came out in sudden rash assertions. "You see that one with the green tie?" he asked in English, pointing at a man across the room. "He's a rotten coward. An MVD. He wants to make me trouble." Or, "I like the West. I have been to Berlin, and met Marlene Dietrich. She was in love with me."

The other couple at the table, a man and wife, were silent until Miss Johnson and the sculptor left to dance. Then the woman, a death-pale brunette with Mongolian cheekbones and green almond eyes, said to me, "What an appalling little man. So dirty. A *Georgian*, of course. These people from the South!" She spoke English with the spurious elegance, the strained exactness of Liza Doolittle. "I am Madame Nervitsky. You of course know my husband, the crooner," she said, introducing me to the gentleman, who was twice her age, somewhere in his sixties, a vain, once-handsome man with an inflated stomach and a collapsing chin line. He wore make-up, powder, pencil, a touch of rouge. He knew no English, but told me in French, "*Je suis* Nervitsky. Le Bing Crosby de Russie." His wife was startled that I'd never heard of him. "No? *Nervitsky*? The famous *crooner*?" Her surprise was justified. In the Soviet Union, Nervitsky is a considerable celebrity, the idol of young girls who swoon over his interpretations of popular ballads. During the twenties and thirties he lived in Paris, enjoying a minor vogue as a cabaret artist. When that faltered, he went on a honkytonk tour of the Far East. Though of Russian parentage, his wife was born in Shanghai, and it was there that she met and married Nervitsky. In 1943, they moved to Moscow, where she launched a not too prosperous career as a film actress. "I am a painter really. But I can't be bothered ingratiating all the right people. That is necessary if you want your pictures shown. And painting is so difficult when one travels." Nervitsky spends most of the year making personal appearances throughout Russia. He was currently engaged for a series of concerts in Leningrad. "Nervitsky is more sold out than the Negroes," his wife informed me. "We are going to the Negro premiere," she said, and added that she was sure it would be a "delightful" evening because "the Negroes are so amusing and there is so little amusing here. Nothing but work, work. We're all too tired to be amusing. Don't you find Leningrad absolutely dead? A beautiful corpse? And Moscow. Moscow is not quite as dead, but so ugly." She wrinkled her nose and shuddered. "I suppose, coming from New York, you find us very shabby? Speak the truth. You think *me* shabby?" I didn't think that, no. She wore a simple black dress, some good jewelry, there was a mink stole slung over her shoulders. In fact, she was the best-dressed, best-looking woman I'd seen in Russia. "Ah, you're embarrassed to say. But I know. When I look at your friends, these American girls, I *feel* shabby. There are no nice things next to my skin. It isn't that I'm poor. I have money . . ." She hesitated. Miss Johnson and the sculptor were returning to the table. "Please," she said, "I would like to say something to you privately. Do you dance?"

The band was smooching its way through "Somebody Loves Me," and the crowd on the floor listened to Lamar rasp out the lyrics with transfixed, transfigured faces. ". . . who can it be oh *may*-be *ba*-by *may*-be it's you!" Madame Nervitsky danced well, but her body was tense, her hands icy. *"J' adore le musique des Negres.* It's so wicked. So vile," she said, and then, in the same breath, began to whisper rapidly in my ear, "You and your friends must find Russia very expensive. Take my advice, don't change your dollars. Sell your clothes. That is the way to get rubles. Sell. Anyone will buy. If it can be done discreetly. I am here in the hotel, Room 520. Tell your friends to bring me shoes, stockings, things for close to the skin. Anything," she said, digging her nails into my sleeve, "tell them I will buy *anything.* Really," she sighed, resuming a normal voice and raising it above the shriek of Mignatt's trumpet, "the Negroes are so delightful."

Somewhat set back from the Nevsky Prospekt, there is an arcaded building bearing a marked resemblance to St. Peter's. This is the Kazin Cathedral, Lenin-

146

grad's largest antireligious museum. Inside, in an atmosphere of stained-glass gloom, the management has produced a Grand Guignol indictment against the teachings of the church. Statues and sinister portraits of the Popes follow each other down the galleries like a procession of witches. Everywhere ecclesiastics leer and grimace, make, in captioned cartoons, satyr suggestions to nunlike women, revel in orgies, snub the poor to cavort with the decadent rich. Ad infinitum the museum demonstrates its favorite thesis: that the church, the Roman Catholic in particular, exists solely as a protection to capitalism. One caricature, an enormous oil, depicts Rockefeller, Krupp, Hetty Green, Morgan and Ford plunging ferocious hands into a mountainous welter of coins and blood-soaked war helmets.

The Kazin Cathedral is popular with children. Understandably so, since the exhibition is liberally sprinkled with horror-comic scenes of brutality and torture. The schoolteachers who herd daily swarms of pupils through the place have difficulty dragging them away from such attractions as The Chamber of the Inquisitors. The Chamber is a real room peopled with the life-sized wax figures of four Inquisitors relishing the agonies of a heretic. The naked victim, chained to a table, is being branded with hot coals by a pair of masked torturers. The coals are electrically lighted. Children, even when pulled away, keep sneaking back for a second look.

Outside the cathedral, on the many columns support-
ing its arcades, there is another kind of display. Coarse
chalk drawings, the usual men's room graffiti, scarcely
worth mentioning, except that it seems on first thought
an odd place to find it; and on second it doesn't. In a
way it belongs.

Antireligious museums were not among the sightsee-
ing projects their hosts had lined up for the *Porgy
and Bess* cast. Quite the contrary, on Sunday, Christmas Day, the Soviets provided the choice of attending a
Catholic Mass or a Baptist service. Eleven members
of the company, including Rhoda Boggs, a soprano
playing the part of the Strawberry Woman, went to
the Baptist Evangelical Church, whose Leningrad pa-
rishioners number two thousand. Afterwards, I saw
Miss Boggs sitting alone in the Astoria dining room.
She is a round, honey-colored, jolly-faced woman, always carefully groomed, but now her little Sunday best
hat was slightly askew, the handkerchief she kept dab-
bing at her eyes was wet as a washcloth.

"I'm tore to pieces," she told me, her breasts heav-
ing. "I've been going to church since I can walk, but
I never felt Jesus like I felt Jesus today. Oh, child, he
was *there*. He was out in the open. He was plainly
written on every face. He was singing with us, and you
never heard such beautiful singing. It was old people
mostly, and old people can't sing like that without
Jesus is helping them along. The pastor, there was a
sweet old man, he asked us colored people would we

render a spiritual, and they listened so quiet, all those rows and rows and rows of old faces just looking at us, like we were telling them nobody's alone when Jesus is everywhere on this earth, which is a fact they know already, but it seemed to me like they were glad to hear it. Anybody doubts the presence of Our Saviour, he should've been there. Well, it came time to go. To say good-bye. And you know what happened? They stood up, the whole congregation. They took out white handkerchiefs and waved them in the air. And they sang, 'God Be With You Till We Meet Again.' The tears were just pouring down our faces, them and ours. Oh, child, it churned me up. I can't keep nothing on my stomach.''

That evening, with the premiere less than twenty-four hours away, the windows of the Astoria stayed lighted late. All night footsteps hurried along the corridors, doors slammed and telephones rang, as though a calamity were happening.

In Suite 415, Ambassador Bohlen and his wife entertained a small group of aides and friends who had just arrived with them by train from Leningrad. The gathering, which included Roye L. Lowry, Second Secretary at the Embassy and one of the two diplomats who had "briefed" the company in Berlin, was exceptionally quiet, since the Bohlens didn't want their presence in the hotel known until the last possible moment. They concealed themselves so successfully that the next morning Warner Watson, believing the diplomatic contingent were coming by plane, set out for the Leningrad airport with a bouquet for Mrs. Bohlen. Directly below the ambassadorial apartment, in Suite 315, Mrs. Breen was seesawing on a Relaxer Board, while her husband polished the pre-curtain speech he planned to deliver. It had been suggested to him that he might circumvent the Communist propaganda potential in *Porgy and Bess* by pointing out that its picture of American Negroes concerned the long ago, not today, and so he added the line, *"Porgy and Bess* is set in the past. It no more reflects the present than if it were about life under the Czars in Russia." In Room 223, Leonard Lyons was at his typewriter outlining the opening-night column he intended cabling his newspaper, the *New York Post.* "On stage were the flags of both nations, the U.S.S.R. and the U.S.A." he wrote, previewing the event. "The last time an American flag was displayed here was when there were only forty-five states in the union. A representative of the Ministry of Culture phoned to inquire how many states are united now. Yesterday a wardrobe mistress sewed three more stars on the old flag." The item finished a page. Lyons inserted a new sheet with fresh carbons. Instead of throwing the old carbon in a wastebasket, he took it to the bathroom and flushed it into oblivion. It was safer, he felt, to destroy used carbons, otherwise the Soviets, or perhaps rival correspondents, might ferret them out and decipher what he was writing.

And indeed, the hotel was seething with journalistic competitors. *The Saturday Evening Post* was there in the person of Charles R. Thayer, Ambassador Bohlen's brother-in-law. Thayer, and C. L. Sulzberger of *The New York Times,* had arrived with the Bohlen party. *The Saturday Review* was sending Horace Sutton, *Time* and *Life* already had a photographer-reporting team on hand, and Mrs. Richard O'Malley, of AP's Moscow bureau, was speeding toward Leningrad aboard the crack Red Arrow Express, the same train which had, the night before, brought CBS correspondent Dan Schorr.

Now, on the second floor, in Room 111, Schorr, a heavy-set bachelor in his middle thirties, was simultaneously trying to correct a manuscript, keep a pipe lighted, and dictate on the telephone to a stenographer in Moscow. "Okay. Here's the story. You put in the slugs. Let's go," he barked, and began to read from typed pages. *"The Porgy and Bess Company comma believed to be the first American theatrical troupe ever to appear in Russia comma will open its Soviet engagement tomorrow night before a selected audience of two thousand two hundred* I repeat two two oh oh *at Leningrad's Palace of Culture comma but off-stage the Negro actors and singers have already scored a smash hit period The sixty members of the cast comma just by being themselves comma have had a tremendous impact on this comma the second largest city in the Soviet Union* . . . that's right, isn't it? It is the second largest?" For twenty minutes more Schorr droned out anecdotes and fact. Long lines of Leningraders had waited all night in the snow to buy tickets at a top-scale of sixty rubles ($15), a price doubled and tripled on the black market. "Hey, what's a synonym for black market that we can get past the censors? Okay, make it curb price." Toward the end, he was saying, *"They have given Leningrad a Christmas probably unlike any in history period Until four o'clock this morning they gathered around a Christmas tree dash provided by a solicitous Soviet government dash and sang carols and spirituals period.* Yeah, I know I'm overfiling this story. But I got excited. Real excited. You can see it. The impact of one culture on another culture. And by the way, listen, I'm having a helluva time. They're a great bunch, these *Porgy and Bess* people. Like living with a circus."

On Monday morning, the day of the premiere, the cast met at Leningrad's Palace of Culture for a final dress rehearsal with full orchestra. Originally the Soviets had intended housing the production in the attractive Mariinsky theatre, but the demand for tickets convinced them they could double their profit by transferring the opera to the huge Palace of Culture. The Palace, a pile of muddy-orange concrete, was slapped together in the thirties. From the outside it is not unlike one of those decaying examples of supermarket architecture along Hollywood and Vine. Several things about the interior suggest a skating rink. Its temperature, for one. But Davy Bey, and the other children in the company, thought it was "a grand place," especially the vast backstage with its black recesses for hiding, its fly ropes to swing on, and where the tough backstage crew, strong men and stronger women, caressed them, gave them candy sticks and called them *"Aluchka,"* a term of affection.

I rode over to the rehearsal in a car shared by two of the Ministry's interpreters, Miss Lydia and the tall, personable youth named Sascha. Miss Lydia, a woman who enjoys her food, was in a fine state of excitement, as though she were about to sit down to a delicious meal. "We will see it, no? Now we will *see* this *Porgy-Bess,"* she said, wiggling on the seat. And then it occurred to me that yes, of course, at last Miss Lydia and her Ministry colleagues would be able to judge for themselves "this *Porgy-Bess,"* the myth that had for so long consumed their hours and energy. Even Savchenko would be having his first glimpse. Here and there along the route, Miss Lydia happily pointed at street placards advertising the show. Breen's name, repeated often, was in bigger, bolder type than Gershwin's, and the name of his absent co-producer, Blevins Davis, was omitted altogether. The day before, Mrs. Gershwin had observed to Warner Watson that in Russia the name Gershwin seemed to be "riding in the rumble seat"; to which Watson had replied, "Look, Lee, it's got to be Robert's show this time. He wants it that way. He's just got to have it."

"How do you sit that still?" Miss Lydia inquired of Sascha. "Now we *see* it. Before the ordinary people." Sascha *was* still. He had a seasick, stricken look, and not without reason. That morning Savchenko had thrown Breen into a tailspin by telling him that the production's theatre programs were still at the printer and would not be obtainable for another few days. It was an authentic crisis because the programs contained a synopsis of the opera's plot, and Breen was afraid that without this guide the audience would have difficulty following the action. Savchenko offered a solution. Why not have one of the Ministry's translators come before the curtain and, prior to each act, outline the plot? Sascha had been chosen for the task. "How will I handle my feet?" he said, his eyes hypnotized with stage fright. "How will I speak when there is no water in my mouth?" Miss Lydia tried to soothe him. "Think only what an honor! Many important people will be present. You will be noticed. If you were *my* son, Sascha, I would be very proud."

Inside the Palace of Culture's darkened auditorium, Sascha and Miss Lydia found seats in the fourth row. I sat down behind them, between Savchenko and "Joe" Adamov, both of whom were exploring their mouths with toothpicks. Other Russians, some thirty-odd who had finagled invitations to watch the run-through, were scattered around in the first several rows. Among them were Moscow journalists and photographers who had come to cover the premiere. The orchestra in the pit, an importation from Moscow's Stanislavski Theatre, was winging through the overture with confident ease. The conductor, Alexander Smallens, a Russian-born American who has made rather a life's work of *Porgy and Bess,* having maestroed its every incarnation, including the original 1935 production, said the Stanislavski was the sixty-first orchestra under his command and the best of the lot. "Superb musicians, and a joy to work with. They love the score, and they have the tempo, the rhythm. All they need now is a little more the *mood.*" On stage, Breen, wearing a beret, a windbreaker, and a pair of close-fitting frontier pants, motioned the cast into place for the first scene. Flat overhead rehearsal lights shadowed the actors' faces, drained the color from the scenery and accentuated its wrinkled wornness. The set, a simple functional job, depicts a corner of Catfish Row with its balconied houses and shuttered windows. Presently, responding to a signal from Breen, a soprano leaned over a balcony and began to sing the opening song, "Summertime." Miss Lydia recognized the melody. She swayed her head and hummed with the music until Savchenko tapped her on the shoulder and growled an admonition that made her shrink in her seat. Midway through the performance, Adamov dug me with his elbow and said,

"I speak pretty good English, right? Well *I* can't figure what the hell they're yelling about. All this dialect crap! I think . . . " but I never heard what he thought, for Savchenko turned round with a look that strangled Adamov. Most of the Russians were as silent as Savchenko could have wished. The rows of profiles, silhouetted in the glow from the stage, remained as severely unmarred by expression as coin engravings. At the end, with the last aria sung, there was a quiet drifting off to the cloakrooms. Savchenko and Miss Lydia, Sascha and two other young men from the Ministry, Igor and Henry, waited together while an attendant brought their coats. I walked over and asked Miss Lydia her opinion of what she'd seen. She bit her lower lip, her eyes darted toward Savchenko, who said firmly, "Interesting. Most interesting." Miss Lydia nodded, but neither she nor Sascha, Igor nor Henry, would venture a different adjective. "Yes," they all said, "interesting. Most interesting."

The average playing time of *Porgy and Bess* is approximately two and a half hours, but this final run-through, involving many pauses for corrections, lasted from 10 A.M. until two in the afternoon. The cast, edgy with hunger and anxious to return to the hotel, were annoyed when, after the theatre had emptied of Russian spectators, Breen informed them that the rehearsal was not yet over. He wanted to re-stage the curtain calls.

As matters stood, and though only the two players

in the title roles took individual bows, the pattern of calls already established required six minutes to complete. Not many productions can expect an audience to sustain six minutes of applause. Breen now proposed extending these six minutes indefinitely by contriving what amounted to "a separate little show. Just," he said, "an impromptu thing. Sort of like an encore." It consisted of having a drummer beat a bongo while, one at a time, every winking, waving member of the company sashayed across the stage inviting individual applause. Even the stage manager, the wardrobe mistress, the electricians, and naturally the director himself, were set to receive homage from the audience. One had the choice of two conclusions: either Breen was counting on an ovation of volcanic vigor, or he feared the reverse, and so was insuring prolonged applause by staging this "impromptu" extra curtain call. Obviously under the delicate diplomatic circumstances, no audience would walk out while the performers were still, in a sense, performing.

Private limousines had been put at the disposal of the leading players. Martha Flowers, who alternates with Ethel Ayler in the role of Bess, and who had been assigned to sing the part that evening, offered me a return ride to the Astoria. I asked if she were nervous about the premiere. "Me? Uh uh. I've been doing this show two years. The only thing makes me nervous is, maybe I'm ruining my voice for serious work." Miss Flowers, a young Juilliard graduate, is ambitious to make a reputation as a concert recitalist. She is small and perky. Whether smiling or not, her lips are always pursed downward, as though she'd just tasted a green persimmon. "I'm tired, though. I sure am that. This kind of climate's no good for a singer. You've really got to watch your throat," she said, massaging her own. "The other Bess, you know—Ethel, she's in bed with a bad cold. Got a temperature and everything. So I'll have to sing the matinée tomorrow and maybe the evening, too. Well, a person could ruin their voice *forever,* carrying on like that." She described her schedule between now and curtain time. "I ought to eat something. But first I'll take a bath. Can you float in your tub? Mine's so big I can float. I'll take a nap, too. We start for the theatre at six. Maybe six-thirty I'll be slipping into my costume and pinning that old red flower in my hair. Then I guess I'll have a long sit."

At six-thirty, the hour when Miss Flowers was presumably in her dressing room pinning on a paper rose, Mrs. Breen and Mrs. Gershwin were in the Bohlens' suite, where they had been asked to have drinks prior to leaving for the Palace of Culture. Breen himself, too busy to accept the Ambassador's hospitality, had already gone to the theatre.

The drinks, Scotch and tap water, were being served by Bohlen's aide, Roye L. Lowry, and Mrs. Lowry, a couple harmoniously matched in their conservative,

schoolteacherish demeanor. Mrs. Bohlen's close
friend, Marina Sulzberger, the quick-witted wife of
the *Times* man, was also present to provide the host-
ess with conversational assistance. Not that Mrs.
Bohlen, a serenely efficient woman with a dairymaid
complexion and sensible blue eyes, gives an impression of being unable to keep any conversation afloat,
however awkward. But there was, if one remembers
the exceedingly reproachful letter Breen had dispatched to Bohlen a few days earlier, a certain awk-
wardness inherent in this meeting between representatives of Everyman Opera and the U. S. State Department. As for the Ambassador, one would not suppose,
from his amiable manner, that he'd ever received
such a letter. A career diplomat for more than twenty-
five years, a large percentage of them spent at the
Moscow Embassy, where he first held Lowry's present post, Second Secretary, and where he was ulti-
mately appointed Ambassador in 1952, Bohlen still
resembles a photograph taken the year (1927) he
graduated from Harvard. Experience has harshened
his sportsman's handsomeness, salted his hair and re-
duced, rather obliterated, a dreaming naïveté around
the eyes. But the direct look of youth, of rugged stam-
ina, has stayed with him. He lounged in his chair, sipping Scotch and talking to Mrs. Breen as though they
were in a country room with a warm hearth and
lazing dogs on the floor.

But Mrs. Breen couldn't relax. She sat on the edge

of her seat, like an applicant for a job. "It's so sweet of you to have come. Just dear of you," she told Bohlen in a small-girl voice that was somehow not quite her own. "It means so much to the cast."

"You don't think we would've *missed* it?" said Bohlen, and his wife added, "Not for anything in the world! It's the high point of the winter. We've thought of nothing else, have we, Chip?" she said, using the Ambassador's nickname.

Mrs. Breen modestly lowered her eyes, a touch of color tinged her cheeks. "It means so much to the cast."

"It means so much to *us*," said Mrs. Bohlen. "Our life isn't so amusing that we could afford to miss something like this. Why, we'd have got here if we'd had to walk the whole way. Crawled on our hands and knees."

Mrs. Breen raised her eyes for an instant, and glanced sharply at the Ambassador's wife, as though half suspecting her of satiric intent; then, reassured by Mrs. Bohlen's straight, clear face, she dropped her gaze again. "It's just dear of you," she whispered. "And of course we're all thrilled about the party in Moscow."

"Oh, yes . . . the party," said Mrs. Bohlen, with detectable resignation. In honor of the company's Moscow premiere, two weeks hence, the Bohlens had promised to give an official reception at their residence, Spaso House.

"Robert and I do hope Mr. Bulganin will be there. We want to thank him personally for all the courtesy we've received. The Ministry of Culture paid Robert a lovely tribute. Seven ivory elephants." Mrs. Breen was referring to a mantelpiece parade of plastic elephants that Savchenko had presented as a gift to Breen.

"How very nice," said Mrs. Bohlen dimly, as though she'd lost the conversational thread. "Well, of course, we can't be quite sure *who's* coming to the party. We're sending out two hundred invitations, more or less, but since Russians never answer an R.S.V.P., we never know who to expect or how many."

"That's right," said the Ambassador. "You don't count on these fellows until they walk in the door. Any of them. And when they give a party themselves they almost never invite you until the last minute. Everyone in the diplomatic corps keeps the evening free when we know there's going to be a big affair at the Kremlin. We just sit around, hoping the phone will ring. Sometimes we're in the middle of dinner before they invite us. Then it's a rush. Fortunately, you never have to dress for these things," he said, reverting to a previous topic, and a painful one for Mrs. Breen, who, earlier in the day, had been chagrined to learn that Bohlen was unwilling to attend the opening in black-tie. Indeed, driven by her determination to "make everything gala," she had gone a step further and envisioned the Ambassador wearing white tie and tails, which is what her husband planned to do. But, "It never occurred to me to bring a dinner jacket," said Bohlen, fingering a button of the dark grey suit he considered proper to the occasion. "No one wears them here. Not even for a premiere."

Over in a corner, Mrs. Gershwin and Mrs. Sulzberger were elaborating on the same sartorial theme. "Of *course* we shouldn't dress up. That's what I've told Wilva all along. We went to a ballet the other night and looked perfectly ridiculous. Oh, there's too much fuss around here. I don't know what the fuss is all about. After all, it's *only* little old *Porgy.*"

"Actually," said Mrs. Sulzberger, a Greek-born woman whose clever eyes sparkle with Mediterranean mischief, "it might not be a bad thing for the Russians to see people dressed. There's no excuse to go about looking the way they do. When we first came here, I felt sorry for them," she said, and added that she and her husband had been in the Soviet Union two weeks, staying as house guests of the Bohlens. "I thought the way they dressed, the dreariness of it all, I imagined it was because they were terribly poor. But really, you know, that's not true. They look this way because they want to. They do it on purpose."

"Yes," said Mrs. Gershwin, "that's what I think."

"I wonder," mused Mrs. Sulzberger. "I wonder. Do you suppose the Russians are so awful because they've always been beaten? Or have they always been beaten because they're so awful?"

"Yes," said Mrs. Gershwin, "that's what I think."

Lowry caught the Ambassador's eye, and glanced significantly at his watch. Outside the hotel a limousine was purring its engine, preparing to carry the Bohlens to the theatre. Other Zivs, a street-long gleam of them, waited for Mrs. Breen and Mrs. Gershwin, for Savchenko and Adamov and the employees of AP, Time-Life, CBS. Soon the cars would start slithering across the square, like a funeral cortege.

Bohlen swallowed his Scotch and accompanied his guests to the door of the suite. "I don't think you have anything to worry about," he told Mrs. Breen. "The Russians are very musical people. You'll have rubles coming out of your ears."

"Adorable man. And she's charming, too," Mrs. Gershwin remarked to Mrs. Breen, as the two ladies descended the stairs.

"Adorable. But," said Mrs. Breen, her shy little-girl voice suddenly maturing, "Robert and I *did* want it to be gala."

"Well, darling, we can't be gala if we're going to be conspicuous," observed Mrs. Gershwin, whose diamonded decorations made her look as though she were moving in a spotlight. "Frankly, myself, I think it would do the Russians a world of good to see people dressed up. There's no excuse for them to go around looking the way they do. When we first came here, I felt sorry for them, but now . . . "

Across town, at the Palace of Culture, snow-sprinkled crowds were massing on the sidewalk to watch the ticket holders arrive, and inside the theatre a sizable number, baking in a blaze of newsreel and television arc lights, were already seated. Baskets of flowers, yellow and white, flanked the stage, and crossed flags, an entwining of stars and stripes and hammer and sickle, floated above the proscenium. Backstage, where the tuning orchestra's chirping flutes and moaning oboes echoed like forest sounds, Martha Flowers, costumed and completely calm, despite the distant, rising audience-roar, was having, as she'd predicted, "a long sit."

And it was very long. The curtain, announced for eight, went up at nine-five and came down at eleven-forty. By midnight I was back at the Astoria waiting for a call from Henry Shapiro, the UP correspondent in Moscow who'd said he would telephone me after the premiere to find out "how it went. What really happened." There is no absolute truth in these matters, only opinion, and as I attempted to formulate my own, tried to decide what I was going to tell Shapiro, I stretched on the bed and switched out the light. My eyes smarted from the recent glare of flash bulbs, I seemed still to hear the soft clickety noise of newsreel cameras. And indeed, lying in the dark, it was as though a film were rushing through my head, a disconnected rampage of pictures: Martha Flowers tripping to the footlights to throw the audience a kiss, Savchenko striding through the lobby listening for comments, the terror in Sascha's eyes, Miss Ryan covering her face with her hands. I made a conscious effort to slow the film down, let it start at the beginning.

It began with the audience, an army standing at solemn attention while the orchestra played the national anthems of the two countries: Savchenko had courteously insisted that ''The Star Spangled Banner'' should be heard first. Then individual faces came into focus: Ambassador and Mrs. Bohlen, the Sulzbergers, the Lowrys, Miss Ryan and Leonard Lyons, all together in a front row. Near them, on a platform extending from the side of the stage, a squadron of photographers waited impatiently until the anthems ended: then the platform resembled a besieged fortress, photographers firing away while assistants reloaded their cameras. Some, like CBS's Dan Schorr, desperately alternated between cameras and tape recorders as they went to work documenting the pre-curtain ceremonies. There was no need for such haste. The speeches, and their translations, lasted an hour.

The Russians were brief enough. Konstantin Sergeev, the dapper young ballet master of the Leningrad Theatre, shook hands with Breen and, speaking into a microphone, said "Dear Brothers in art, welcome. We in the Soviet Union have always paid attention and tribute to the art of the United States. We know and cherish the works of such fine artists as Mark Twain, Walt Whitman, Harriet Beecher Stowe, Jack London, and Paul Robeson. We appreciate the talents of George Gershwin, and that is why this meeting is so joyous." Afterwards, apropos of this speech, Mrs. Gershwin said, "I thought I'd faint when I heard the name Gershwin being lumped in with all those Communists."

Breen bowed to Sergeev, and stepped up to the microphone, a preening, impeccable figure in his trim tuxedo and starched shirt. "He just lost his nerve," said Miss Ryan, explaining why at the last minute her employer had abandoned the idea of wearing white tie and tails. But now, watching Breen react to the applause that greeted him, one wouldn't have guessed there was a nerve in his system. His smooth blond face, bleached by the strong lights and exploding flash bulbs, possessed an inward-gazing remoteness, as though he had for so long dreamed the scene before him that it was still a dream; and when he spoke, the measured, sepulchral timbre of his actor's voice strengthened the impression that he thought himself alone on an empty stage addressing an imaginary audience, practicing, as it were, for an ego-satisfying moment that would someday come true. Imaginary audiences are notoriously submissive; but the Palace of

Culture assemblage began to grow talkative themselves as Breen rambled on, the Russian translator trailing behind him. With graceful, *grand seigneur* sweepings of the hand, he introduced Ambassador and Mrs. Bohlen, who rose in their seats to acknowledge applause. The Ambassador had been expected to deliver a speech, but much to Bohlen's relief, and Breen's regret, the Soviets, extremely sensitive to protocol, had asked that this part of the program be deleted because they had no one of "comparable eminence" to make, on the Russian behalf, a rejoinder. Mrs. Gershwin was also introduced, and the conductor, Alexander Smallens, who received a sumptuous hand when Breen announced that Smallens was "born right here in Leningrad." The introductions continued as Breen presented members of the cast who were not performing that evening: Ethel Ayler, the alternate Bess, sufficiently recovered from her cold to have climbed out of bed and into a skimpy, strapless blue gown. And Lorenzo Fuller, the alternate Sportin' Life. Fuller had a "few" words to say, among them a Russian phrase he'd memorized, "*Dobro poshlavat, druzya,*" which means "Welcome, friends." The audience roared approval. But as clock hands crept toward nine, even the frenzied photographers paused to consult watches. "Jesus," said one correspondent, "they ought to have a gong around here. Like Major Bowes." It was as though Breen had overheard him, for abruptly the ceremonial group vacated the stage.

The theatre grew quieter than a hens' roost at sunset as the audience settled back, confident that now the curtain would rise and reveal what they'd paid their rubles to see, *Porgy and Bess*. Instead, Sascha appeared. He crossed the stage stiff-legged and wobbly, as though he were walking a plank. A sheaf of typewritten pages quivered in his hands, and his face, bloodlessly pallid, was drenched with sweat. The instant the audience caught wind of why he was there, to read them the opera's plot, the hens' roost turned into a hornets' nest. They couldn't tolerate another syllable *about* the show, they simply wanted to see it; and a mutiny that broke out in the balcony, where rude voices started shouting, spread to the orchestra: the patrons clapped, whistled, stamped their feet. "Poor Sascha, oh, poor boy," said Miss Ryan, covering her face with her hands. "It's too terrible. I can't bear to watch." Several rows back of Miss Ryan, Sascha's two friends, Igor and Henry, slumped on their spines, but Miss Lydia, less squeamish, glared round at her neighbors, as though she'd like to crack them with her pocketbook. On stage, Sascha went on reading, mumbling, as if he were whispering a prayer against the deafening tumult; like Breen before him, he seemed locked in a dream, a numbing, naked-in-the-street nightmare. Smallens flicked his baton, and the overture sounded as Sascha retreated into the wings.

It was soon evident that the audience regretted not

having paid more attention to Sascha's resumé of the two-act tale the opera tells. In skeleton, the story is this: a crippled begger, Porgy, falls in love with a Charleston tart, Bess. Alas, this neurotic young woman is under the wicked influence of two other gentlemen. One, the devilish dope peddler, Sportin' Life, has enticed her into drug addiction, while the second, an alluringly muscular criminal named Crown, monopolizes the heroine's libidinous impulses. Porgy dispenses of the latter rival by killing him, and when he is sent to jail for the deed, Bess alleviates her woes by going on a dope binge, during which Sportin' Life persuades her to forget Porgy and traipse off with him to New York: "That's where we belong, sister," he sings as they head for the sugary lights of Harlem. In the last scene, Porgy, acquitted of Crown's murder, sets out for the North in a goat-drawn cart, believing, and leaving the spectator to believe, that he will find Bess and bring her home. Although this narrative line seems straight as a ruler, the intricate vocal-choreographic terms in which it is developed would confuse any audience where the language barrier is present, particularly if the music, the style of dancing, the directorial approach are each and all virgin territory, as they were to the overwhelming majority of those assembled in the Palace of Culture.

"Summertime" ended, and there was no applause. The entrance of Porgy went unheralded. Leslie Scott, playing the part, finished "A Woman Is a Sometimes

Thing,'' and paused for the acclaim the number ordinarily arouses. The fact that none came caused a temporary lapse of stage action. Recovering, the cast launched into a jazzy crap-game sequence: whispering ran through the audience, as though they were asking each other what it meant, these excited men tossing dice? The whispering gathered momentum and turned into gasps, a tremor of shock, when Bess, making her initial appearance, hiked up her skirt to adjust her garter. Miss Ryan observed to Mrs. Lowry, ''If they think *that's* so daring, just wait.'' The words weren't out of her mouth before Sportin' Life's witty, lascivious gyrations ignited fresh firecrackers of audible astonishment. The crap game concludes with Crown killing one of Porgy's neighbors; a funeral scene follows: while the murdered man's widow sings a lament, ''My Man's Gone Now,'' the mourning inhabitants of Catfish Row sway in a tribal circle around the corpse. At this point, an important Soviet dignitary turned to a correspondent and said in Russian, ''Ah, now I see! They are going to *eat* him.'' The deceased, undevoured, was trundled off to his grave, and the opera progressed to Porgy's optimistic ''I've Got Plenty of Nothin'.'' Scott, a big and solidly constructed baritone, belted it across the footlights with a fervor that should've stopped the show. It didn't.

The audience's persistent silence seemed not altogether attributable to apathy; rather, for the most part, it appeared to be the result of troubled concentration, an anxious desire to understand; and so, fearful of missing the essential phrase, the significant clue that would unmask the mysteries confronting them, they listened and watched with the brooding intentness of students in a lecture hall. But the first act was almost over before the warmth that comes with comprehension wafted through the theatre. It was created by "Bess, You Is My Woman Now," a duet sung by the two principals: suddenly it was clear that Porgy and Bess were in love, that their song was a tender rejoicing, and the audience, rejoicing too, deluged the performers with applause that was brief but heavy, like tropic rain. However, the drought set in again as the music segued into the jamboree fanfare of "I Can't Sit Down," the first-act finale. The scene is peppered with folklorish humor; and, occasionally, isolated chuckles, lonely-sounding patches of laughter, indicated there were persons who appreciated it. The curtain descended. Silence. The house lights began to come up; the audience blinked, as though until this instant they hadn't known the act was over. They caught their breath, like passengers at the end of a roller-coaster ride, and began to applaud. The applause lasted thirty-two seconds.

"They're stunned," said Lowry, parroting the words, though somehow transforming the spirit, of Breen's prophecy. "They've never seen anything like it."

If the Russians were stunned, they were not alone.

Several of the American journalists huddled together, comparing notes. "It's not going over," a baffled Dan Schorr complained to a bewildered Time-Life photographer. And Mrs. Bohlen, following her husband up the aisle, was poignantly pensive. Later, she told me the thought behind the expression: "I was thinking— well, we've laid an egg. Now what are we going to do about it?"

Out in the crowded lobby, Mrs. Breen smilingly expressed sentiments of a sunnier nature; according to her, the performance was going "beautifully." A correspondent interposed to ask why, in that case, the Russians were "sitting on their hands." Mrs. Breen stared at the questioner as though she thought him certifiable. "But they aren't *supposed* to applaud," she said. "Robert *planned* it that way. So that there wouldn't *be* any applause. It interrupts the mood."

The Wolferts agreed with Mrs. Breen; they felt the premiere was turning out a triumph. "First time we've seen the show," said Wolfert. "I don't like musicals. Got no use for them. But this one's pretty good."

Another American, the Russian-speaking Priscilla Johnson, spent the intermission eavesdropping on the customers. "They're quite shocked," she reported. "They think it's awfully immoral. But gosh, you can't blame them for not liking it. It's such a second-rate production. That's what makes me sad. If only it were *really* good, then you could blame them. Too bad, too

bad," she said, ruffling her bangs, shaking her head.
"This whole setup: the Breens, the publicity and all
—gosh, it's just not geared for failure."

Like Miss Johnson, Savchenko and Adamov circu-
lated about sampling opinions. "It's a very big success," was all Savchenko would admit; but Adamov,
whose slang was growing richer under the company's
tutelage, said: "So a lot of squares don't dig it. They
don't flip. So is that big news? You got squares in
New York, ain'tcha, man?"

Madame Nervitsky and her crooner-husband passed
by. "Oh, we're amazed," she told me, flourishing a
sword-length cigarette holder. "Nervitsky thinks it
très dépravé. Not I. I adore the vileness of it all. The
rhythm, the sweat. Really, the Negroes are too amusing. And how wonderful their teeth!" Moving closer,
she said, "You did tell your friends? Room 520. Don't
telephone, come quietly, bring anything. I will pay
very well."

Stefan Orlov was standing at a refreshment counter,
a glass of mineral water in his hand. "My friend," he
said, clapping me on the shoulder. "What a night we
had, yes? The next morning, my wife, she had to beat
me out of bed. Tie my shoes and knot my tie. Not
angry, you understand: laughing at me." He produced
a pair of opera glasses, and peered through them. "I
saw Nancy. I wondered, should I try to speak to her?
But I said to myself: no, Nancy is sitting with fash-
ionable people. Will you tell her that I saw her?" I

173

said I would, and asked if he was enjoying *Porgy and Bess*. "I wish I had a ticket for every night. It's an experience. Powerful! Like Jack London. Like Gogol. I will never forget it," he said, pocketing the opera glasses. A frown creased his forehead, he opened his mouth to speak, changed his mind, took a swallow of water instead, then changed his mind again, and decided to tell me: "The question isn't whether I forget. Or what we old ones think. It's the young people who matter. It matters that they have new seeds planted in their hearts. Tonight," he said, looking round the lobby, "all these young people will stay awake. Tomorrow, they'll be whistling the music. A nuisance, humming in the classrooms. And in the summer, that's what you'll hear: young people whistling along the river. They won't forget."

Backstage, a tranquil climate prevailed as the performers readied themselves for the second act. Leslie Scott, not the least unnerved by the reception of the previous stanza, grinned and said, "Sure, they're kinda slow. But most audiences don't warm up until the duet ("Bess, You Is My Woman Now"), and that went over okay. From here on out, we'll sail." Martha Flowers, freshening her make-up in front of a mirror, said, "This audience, that audience, I don't know the difference. You wouldn't either, you been doing this show two years." But Sascha, lacking Miss Flowers' professional *savoir*, was an alarming sight as he waited in the wings to repeat his role of plot narrator: head bowed, and holding to a dancer's practice bar like a fighter on the ropes, he listened dazedly while his seconds, Igor and Henry, whispered encouragement.

To Sascha's surprise, his return bout was victorious. The audience was eager to hear what would happen in the next act, and Sascha, who two weeks later applied to the Moscow Art Theatre for a drama student fellowship, ecstatically recounted Crown's murder and Porgy's imprisonment. He walked off to one of the largest hands of the evening; Miss Lydia was still clapping after the house lights had dimmed.

The element in the opera which seemed most to disturb the Soviets, its sensuality, reaches a peak of Himalayan proportions in the opening twenty minutes of Act Two. A song, "I Ain't Got No Shame" ("doin' what I likes to do"), and the shake-that-thing brand of choreography accompanying it, proved too aptly titled, too graphically illustrated, for Russian comfort. But it was the ensuing scene which contained, from a prudish viewpoint, the real affront. The scene, a favorite of the director's and one he'd kept heightening in rehearsal, begins with Crown attempting to rape Bess —he grips her to him, gropes her buttocks, her breasts; and ends with Bess raping him—she rips off his shirt, wraps her arms around him and writhes, sizzles like bacon in a skillet: blackout. Areas of the audience suffered something of a blackout, too. "Christ," said one correspondent, his voice carrying in the hush, "they wouldn't get away with that on Broadway!"

To which another American journalist, a woman, replied: "Don't be silly. It's the best thing in the show."

Leslie Scott had predicted the second act would "sail"; his forecast was almost verified during the opera's remaining forty minutes. The street-cry song of the Strawberry Woman started favorable winds blowing. Again, like the love duet, the melody and the situation, simply a peddler selling strawberries, was one the Russians could grasp, be charmed by. After that, every scene seemed to be accepted; and though the performance did not sail, perhaps because too much water had already been shipped, at least it floated, wallowed along in a current of less frigid temperature.

As the curtain fell, and the calls commenced, cameramen, scooting up and down the aisles, divided their shots between applauding Russians and salaaming actors. "They're stunned," Lowry once more pronounced, and his wife tacked on the inevitable, "They've never seen anything like it." The applause, which one experienced witness described as "nothing compared to an opening night at the Bolshoi," sustained a logical number of curtain calls, then swiftly declined. It was now, when people were leaving their seats, that Breen made his bid for a more impressive demonstration by unleashing the extra-added, "impromptu" curtain call he'd rehearsed that afternoon. On came the cast, one by one, each of them cavorting to the beat of a bongo drum. "Oh, no," groaned Miss Ryan. "They shouldn't do this. It's just begging." In the endurance test that followed, the audience compromised by substituting a chantlike pattern of clapping for authentic applause. Three minutes passed; four, five, six, seven. At last, when Miss Flowers had blown a final kiss across the footlights, and the electricians, et al, had been acknowledged, Breen, taking the ultimate bow, permitted the curtain to be lowered.

Ambassador and Mrs. Bohlen, and various Soviet officials, were ushered backstage to shake hands with the cast. "I don't know what all the fuss is about," Mrs. Gershwin gaily cried as she squeezed through the backstage pandemonium. "It's *only* little old *Porgy*." Savchenko pushed toward Mrs. Breen; stiffly offering his hand, he said, "I want to congratulate you on a very big success." Mrs. Breen dabbed at her eyes, as though drying phantom tears. "That ovation. Wasn't it glorious?" she said, turning to gaze at her husband, who was posing for a photograph with Bohlen. "Such a tribute to Robert."

Outside, I had to walk some distance before finding a taxi. A threesome, two young men and a girl, walked ahead of me. I gathered they'd been part of the *Porgy and Bess* audience. Their voices reverberated down the shadowed, snow-silent streets. They were all talking at once, an exhilarated babble now and again mixed with humming: the strawberry street cry, a phrase of "Summertime." Then, as though she had no true understanding of the words but had memorized them phonetically, the girl sang: "There's a boat that's leavin' soon for New York, come with me, that's where we belong, sister . . ." Her friends joined in, whistling. Orlov had said, "And in the summer, that's what you'll hear: young people whistling along the river. They won't forget."

The promise of these young people who wouldn't forget, who'd been stimulated into new visions: surely, I thought, that was enough to justify my telling Henry Shapiro the premiere was a success. Not the "bombshell" conquest the proprietors of Everyman Opera had expected; but a victory of finer significance, one that would mature and matter. And yet, as I lay in my room thinking it over, qualms seized me when eventually the telephone rang. "How did it go? What really happened?" were questions to be answered on journalism's unsubtle level. Could I, with any honesty, give Shapiro a radiant account of the opera's overall reception? I preferred to; and suspected that it was what he, quite naturally, wanted to hear. But I let the telephone ring while a plethora of *ifs* plunged around in my head: if the Russians had been able to consult a printed program, if the fanfare and ceremonial aspects had been curtailed, if less had been demanded of the audience, if . . . I quit stalling and picked up the receiver. But the person on the line was Miss Lydia, who said she was sorry, someone had called me from Moscow and been disconnected. I had no more calls that evening.

Reviews of the production were published by two of the city's leading papers, *Smena* and *Evening Leningrad*. In Ambassador Bohlen's opinion, the articles were: "By and large, really excellent. Very thoughtful. It shows they took it seriously."

The *Evening Leningrad* critic wrote: "*Porgy and Bess* is a work stamped with brilliant talent and unusual mastery . . . warmly received by the audience." A further fifteen hundred words elaborated on that statement. He praised the score ("Gershwin's music is melodic, sincere, intentionally suffused with Negro musical folklore. There are plenty of really expressive and contrasting melodies."), Breen's direction ("The show is directed with great mastery and rivets one's attention with its dynamic sweep."), the conductor ("The musical part of the performance is on a very high level."), and the cast (" . . . plays together with a harmony rarely to be seen . . ."). The libretto, however, provoked a gentle reprimand, for the writer noticed in it "some elements of expressionism and melodrama, an abundance of the customary details regarding criminal investigation." Nor did *Evening Leningrad* forget to press the political pedal: "We, the Soviet spectators, realize the corrosive effect of the capitalistic system on the consciousness, the mentality and the moral outlook of a people oppressed by poverty. This lifts Heyward's play, as set to music by Gershwin, into the realms of social drama." But such comments seemed a mere pianissimo compared to the loud chords of propaganda that opponents of the *Porgy and Bess* tour had anticipated.

The second critic, U. Kovalyev, writing in *Smena,* mentioned a factor ignored by *Evening Leningrad.* "The astoundingly erotic coloring of some of the dancing scenes is unpleasant. And it is hard to lay the blame on a specific national dance. It is more the taste of the director and perhaps his kind of 'tradition' stemming from Broadway 'burlesques' and 'revues.' But on the whole," continues Kovalyev, *"Porgy and Bess* presents one of the most interesting events of this theatrical season. It is an excellently performed production, colorful, full of movement and music. It testifies to the high talent of the Negro people. Very possibly not all of the music and the staging will be approved by the Soviet audiences and everything will not necessarily be understandable to them. We are not used to the naturalistic details in the dance, to the excessive jazz sound of the symphony orchestra, etc. Nevertheless the performance broadens our concept of the art of contemporary America, and familiarizes us with thus far unknown facets of the musical and theatrical life of the United States."

These reviews did not appear until Thursday, three days after the opening. By then, their publication was rather an anticlimax and the company was inclined to regard them with a yawn. "Sure it's nice they write okay things, but who cares?" said one member of the cast, expressing a prevalent attitude. "It's not what the Russians think. It's the stuff they're hearing about us back home. *That's* what counts."

The company was already aware of what America was hearing, for late Tuesday afternoon, the day following the premiere, Breen received a cable on the subject from Everyman Opera's New York office. Miss Ryan typed copies of it, and she was about to put one of them on the company's bulletin board when we met in the lobby. "Hi," she said. "Guess what? Stefan the Bunny called. He wants to take me dancing. Do you think it'll be all right? I mean, as long as he just wants to dance? Anyway, I don't care. I'd go dancing with Jack the Ripper, anything to get away from *Porgy and Bess*," she said, and thumbtacked her typewritten version of the cable to the bulletin board.

LT ROBERT BREEN HOTEL ASTORIA LENINGRAD USSR

WONDERFUL ARTICLES HERE ALL DECEMBER 27 PAPERS STOP ALL MENTION TEN MINUTES STANDING OVATION STOP

JOURNALS HEADLINE—"LENINGRAD GOES WILD OVER PORGY AND BESS" STOP

AP FACTUAL RELEASE INCLUDES GREAT TICKET DEMAND AND SIZE AUDIENCE STOP

TRIBUNE STRESSES WARM AUDIENCE RECEPTION STOP

TELEGRAM HEADLINE—"PORGY WINS PRAISE FROM RUSSIA" OVER AP RELEASE STOP

MIRROR EDITORIAL "HEART TO HEART DIPLOMACY
—CAST TAKING LENINGRAD BY SONG. WE ARE PROUD OF
THEM" STOP

AP RELEASE IN SOME PAPERS SAYS MOSCOW RADIO
TERMED PREMIERE GREAT SUCCESS STOP

TIMES EDITORIAL TODAY BY SULZBERGER "PORGY BESS
OPENING ANOTHER WINDOW TO WEST"

JOURNAL EDITORIAL TODAY—"MADE TREMENDOUS
HIT"

NBC CBS NEWSCASTS FABULOUS
CONGRATULATIONS TO EVERY SINGLE SOUL WITH YOU

"Of course," remarked Miss Ryan, perusing the
cable, "that's not *exactly* how it arrived. The Breens
did a little adding and editing. There was one line:
'*Times* says scored moderate success.' You can bet
Wilva cut that out! Well," she said with a smile, a sigh,
"why not make a good thing better? Wilva just wants
everybody to feel wonderful, and I think that's kind
of endearing."

All afternoon members of the company, passing
through the lobby, stopped to read the message from
New York. It made them grin, they walked away with
lightened steps. "What'cha say, man?" said Earl
Bruce Jackson to Warner Watson as they stood reading the cable. "We're making history!" And Watson,
rubbing his hands together, replied: "Yep, uh huh. I
guess we've got *history* fenced in."

MODERN LIBRARY PAPERBACKS

THE MODERN LIBRARY, Inc., 457 Madison Ave., N. Y. 22, N. Y.

Interior by Melanie Kahane, A. I. D.

No modern library is complete

without THE AMERICAN

COLLEGE DICTIONARY

1472 pages • 7″ x 10″ • large, clear type, Buckram binding, thumb-indexed $6.00
Buckram binding, without index, $5.00 • Special red Fabrikoid binding, in hand-
some gift box, $7.50 • De luxe red leather binding, gold edges, gift box, $15.00

DAT